The Assertive Woman

by Stanlee Phelps and Nancy Austin

Published by IMPACT and
printed in the United States of America by

BookCrafters
FREDERICKSBURG, VIRGINIA 22401

Table of Contents

Dedication

. . . for our mothers, Connie Phelps and Marilyn Austin, with much love.

Acknowledgements

We sincerely appreciate the enthusiasm and support of Bob Alberti, who initially encouraged us to write this book, along with Mike Emmons. We found their warmth and sincerity to be a rare and cherished gift. Their sensitivity to our ideas and respect for our goals was deeply felt by us.

We also want to thank Lach MacDonald for his perceptive editorial input, as well as for the enjoyment of our mutual consciousness raising.

Also, we want to acknowledge others whose work has influenced us, in particular Sherwin Cotler, Julio Guerra and Robert Liberman, as well as those listed in our bibliography.

A special word of thanks goes to our dear friend, Phyllis Cool, who supported us on many levels from the beginning.

We want to thank Carole Hall for her work in preparing the original manuscript.

We also wish to express our sincere appreciation to the many women who have participated in our workshops. We thank them for their interest, support and encouragement.

S.P.
N.A.

Preface

We have no business writing a preface for *The Assertive Woman*. After all, we are not women, and if there is anything assertive women do *not* need it is to lean on men!

Yet we have a legitimate purpose in these words, both as publishers and as proponents of assertion. In the five years since *Your Perfect Right* was first published, the movement of, by, and for women to achieve independent, assertive personhood has been nothing short of phenomenal. Indeed, although we have been told that some women find *Your Perfect Right* to be sexist (partially in the use of masculine pronouns), we know that much of the success of IMPACT'S first book has been due to its adoption by women as a guidebook for personal growth in assertiveness.

Now, *The Assertive Woman* will be available to fill that role more adequately and appropriately. Stanlee Phelps and Nancy Austin have developed a comprehensive manifesto for the individual woman's achievement of personal power. They speak directly to the woman who finds herself bound by the sexist, oppressive, "put down" aspects of the culture in which we live. They present a clearly-written manual for systematic attack upon the self-denying life style so many women have been conditioned to accept. The steps they suggest are based upon proven principles, and they will work for you.

Our enthusiasm for *The Assertive Woman* reflects our belief in the basic human rights of all persons. Our premise is that all people are equal on a human-to-human level. Although one's boss may be "above" in role, the boss has no right to mistreat the employee. Male "superiority" in the family has the strength of historical "tradition" in supporting the denial of equal rights for other family members. Women have been carefully taught to be submissive, coy, and devious in expressing their feelings; they are systematically reinforced for denying themselves ("After all, that's a woman's *role*, isn't it?") We have observed many who have suffered extreme emotional and physical pain from such self-denial. Who can reckon the loss to our society of the potential contribution of women who have learned this self-inhibiting role too well?

We note a common concern among our "fellow men" (and some traditional women as well): that the message of self-assertion for women will produce a generation of women who will upset established relationships. If so, and we have little doubt that some relationships *will* be threatened by the concept of equality, we submit that these relationships were on shaky ground to begin with. As men, we have found *The Assertive Woman* of great help in our understanding of "where women are coming from." This book will foster better understanding and communication between the sexes, because it facilitates *honesty* and *equality*.

Men will find help here in answering the age-old sexist question: "Why can't a woman be more like a man?" *The Assertive Woman* answers clearly: She need not and ought not be like anyone or anything except *who she truly is*. When a woman is genuinely being herself, not hiding behind non-assertive, or aggressive styles, or burdened under the trappings of a male-dominated society, both sexes stand to benefit.

This work is not aimed at the extremes of the "feminist movement" or the "ultra-feminine woman" point of view. Phelps and Austin have instead presented a style of *individual choice*. As men, however, sexist and chauvinistic we may be, we admire, respect and love assertive women. A person who has high self-regard, a positive sense of personal value, a capacity for independence (whether of men or of movements of other external forces) is our idea of the assertive woman. She can *choose* to select her own styles or not, to go first or not, to do her own thing or to support someone else's thing. In short, she is free *to be herself*, and to choose any course of action which may appeal to her.

We encouraged Stanlee and Nancy from the early work on their manuscript, and are extremely pleased to be publishers of *The Assertive Woman*. Our association with them has been rewarding and enjoyable for us all. We think all readers will find the result rewarding and enjoyable as well.

Robert E. Alberti, Ph.D.
Michael L. Emmons, Ph.D.

Introduction

Just as a bird that flies about
And beats itself against the cage,
Finding at last no passage out
It sits and sings, and so overcomes its rage.
—Abraham Cowley (1618-1667)

Women of the 70's are caught between conforming to existing standards or role definitions and exploring the promise of new alternatives. Inevitably there is an imbalance as women begin to choose new alternatives and attempt to integrate them into the security of established conventions. Husbands may object to a wife choosing to attend a class rather than staying home to cook dinner; prospective employers may hesitate to hire a qualified woman because of her "family obligations"; we write with a sense of the personal frustration felt by women who have been told they have unlimited freedom but whose options are, in fact, limited. We are concerned with the feelings of anxiety, helplessness and powerlessness that prevent a woman from choosing for herself, from expressing her feelings directly and spontaneously, and from having the confidence to ask for what she needs and wants.

In anxiety-provoking situations, many women feel unable to act. They find themselves at a loss to come up with an effective response, or any response at all. In this book we present new alternative solutions for many familiar problems. This book is designed to teach women to develop assertive skills to complement their heightened awareness of changing values and roles. The assertive woman learns to overcome or to reduce the anxiety that often accompanies the making of significant change.

Dr. Robert E. Alberti and Dr. Michael L. Emmons in *Your Perfect Right* define assertive behavior as behavior that allows a person to express honest feelings comfortably, to be direct and straightforward, and to exercise personal rights without denying the rights of others and without experiencing undue anxiety or guilt. A non-assertive person expends much energy in avoiding conflicts, manipulating others, and denying responsibility for her or his own actions. On the other hand, the aggressive person may act to resolve conflicts or to achieve goals but, in the process, violate the rights of others.

The assertive woman recognizes the importance of behavioral changes as well as changes in her thoughts, feelings, and beliefs. She learns each unit of behavior so that she can fit the pieces together gradually as she practices new assertive behaviors. Becoming assertive is like learning to drive a car or to play tennis: there are several behaviors that you will have to coordinate in order to develop an assertive body image that will match your new assertive words. You will have to remind yourself constantly, "I will become as skilled at asserting myself as Billie Jean King is at playing at tennis, if I practice it as diligently!"

This book will help you to integrate these new skills without experiencing undue anxiety or nervousness. It provides you with guidelines for relaxation and other exercises intended to help you to act assertively in a variety of situations. We ask that you consider thinking and talking about some of the changing values and roles of women in society today. We will explore whether or not some of our traditional values and stereotypes still serve a useful purpose for you as an individual.

We hope that this book becomes a personal friend to you. Our suggestions are a friend's suggestions. You don't have to accept a friend's suggestion at face value; you listen, you think, you choose what seems best for you and you discard the rest. After all, that's being assertive!

Overall, several areas of concern repeatedly emerge when women are learning to become assertive. We feel that each of these areas is important enough to warrant a special chapter, presented in the same order we use in our workshops. In Chapter II, "Your Body" and Chapter III, "Your Mind" we offer background in the basic concepts and behaviors involved in learning to be an assertive woman.

The ensuing chapters deal with actual situations which cause pain to many women as they try to assert themselves. Finally, we discuss possible applications and implications of acting assertively. We concern ourselves with the role of consciousness-raising groups in fostering enlightened awareness and mutual support. With this book and with such support, women can translate awareness into behavior. You can answer the question, "OK, I know I've been oppressed, *now* what do I do?"

Who will benefit from this book?

First of all, women will benefit most directly from this book, and because of their interdependency with children and men, there will be indirect benefits for society at large. In this sense, we believe that learning to act assertively can be a central part of the liberation of all human beings. Because the socialization process begins at birth, rigid sexual and racial stereotypes and roles are imposed upon people even before they are aware of their ability to develop options. Many of us grow up unaware of our right to choose for ourselves and our right to reject culturally imposed customs.

We write this book in a very personal, rather than a technical, style, because we intend it for *all* women, *all* ages, *all* colors. Regardless of whether a woman chooses to be a homemaker and/or a career person, or chooses to try a new life style, or live in another country—we strongly believe that the woman as a person must come first. The question of identity is an important one: whether you identify yourself as a mother, a feminist, a student, a lover, an executive, a rebel, a girl, a socialist or a divorcee—if you can put the word "assertive" before any of those identities, you will feel and convey strength no matter who you are or what you are trying to accomplish. This book was written for you, the individual woman, the assertive woman.

Many books and magazines written for women have been criticized for appealing only to a limited audience. Factions of the

Women's Movement have emerged, and people point their fingers and say, "See, even Women's Liberation isn't united." In fact, throughout history people have been subjected to divide-and-conquer tactics. We have been taught to put someone else down in order to elevate ourselves. Women especially have been caught in this role and are expected to be "catty and competitive" with each other.

Through our book we hope to begin to weave a thread of unity among women in the hope that learning to be assertive will be the concern of all. Assertion is as basic as food, shelter, and love. Without these basics, there is an eventual death—either physical, spiritual or emotional.

How to use this book as a workbook.

Throughout this book, several exercises have been included for you to complete. Some of the exercises require only a written response, and others involve actually performing new behaviors. We use all of the exercises in our workshops and have found them to be most effective aids to learning assertive behavior.

We suggest that you complete each exercise in the order in which it is presented. Some of the exercises are designed for you to complete alone. Others are intended to be completed with a friend, and several work best when used as group exercises.

The exercise pages may be copied for use in groups or workshops, provided they are not sold commercially, and that credit is given.

Do you know your AQ?

You may ask yourself, do I really need to read *The Assertive Woman?* Test your assertiveness quotient (AQ) by completing the following questionnaire. Use the scale below to indicate how comfortable you are with each item:

    1—makes me very uncomfortable
    2—I feel moderately comfortable
    3—I am very comfortable with this

There may be some situations which are not relevant to you nor to your particular lifestyle; in such cases, try to imagine how comfortable you might feel if you were involved in the situation.

Since some of our workshops have included men, some of the men have found it interesting to test their own assertiveness by taking the AQ Test and relating their responses to their own experiences or those of women they know. Thus, the AQ Test can be a non-threatening way to initiate discussions between women and men.

AQ Test

Assertive Behaviors

- Speaking up and asking questions at a meeting _____
- Commenting about being interrupted by a male directly to him at the moment he interrupts you _____
- Stating your views to a male authority figure, (e.g., minister, boss, therapist, father) _____
- Attempting to offer solutions and elaborating on them when there are men present _____

Your Body

- Entering and exiting a room where men are present _____
- Speaking in front of a group _____
- Maintaining eye contact, keeping your head upright, and leaning forward when in a personal conversation _____

Your Mind

- Going out with a group of friends when you are the only one without a "date" _____
- Being especially competent, using your authority and/or power without labeling yourself as "bitchy, impolite, bossy, aggressive, castrating, or parental" _____
- Requesting expected service when you haven't received it (e.g. in a restaurant or a store) _____

Apology

- Being expected to apologize for something and *not* apologizing since you feel you are right _____

- Requesting the return of borrowed items without being apologetic _____

Compliments, Criticism, and Rejection

- Receiving a compliment by saying something assertive to acknowledge that you agree with the person complimenting you _____
- Accepting a rejection _____
- Not getting the *approval* of the most significant male in your life and/or of *any* male _____
- Discussing another person's criticism of you openly with that person _____
- Telling someone that she/he is doing something that is bothering you _____

Saying "No"

- Refusing to get coffee or to take notes at a meeting where you are chosen to do so because you are a female _____
- Saying "no"—refusing to do a favor when you really don't feel like it _____
- Turning down a request for a meeting or date _____

Manipulation and Counter-Manipulation

- Telling a person when you think she/he is manipulating you _____
- Commenting to a male who has made a patronizing remark to you (e.g., "you have a good job *for a woman*"; "you're not flighty, emotional, stupid, or hysterical like *most women*") _____

Sensuality

- Telling a prospective lover about your physical attraction to him/her before any such statements are made to you _____
- Initiating sex with your partner _____
- Showing physical enjoyment of an art show or concert

in spite of others' reactions _____
• Asking to be caressed and/or telling your lover what
feels good to you _____

Anger

• Expressing anger directly and honestly when you feel
angry _____
• Arguing with another person _____

Humor

• Telling a joke _____
• Listening to a friend tell a story about something
embarrassing, but funny, that you have done _____
• Responding with humor to someone's put-down of you _____

Children

• Disciplining your own children _____
• Disciplining others' children _____
• Explaining the facts of life or your divorce to your
child _____

Women Together

• Talking about your feelings of competition with another
woman with whom you feel competitive _____

Though our AQ Test is not a validated psychological scale or
test, you can use it to help you discover in what areas you are not
assertive. If you have 1's and 2's under a particular heading, be sure
to give special attention to the corresponding chapter. If you have
more 1's and 2's throughout the AQ Test than you do 3's, *The
Assertive Woman* can help you to become a more spontaneous and
honest person. For those of you who have thirty or more 3's—
congratulations! You already are an assertive woman. We especially
recommend reading Chapter XIV "Freedom" and putting your
assertiveness to work for yourself and others.

Although our book is intended to be read in sequence, you may choose to concentrate on some areas that relate more to your individual needs as highlighted by your AQ score. In fact, after reading *The Assertive Woman* and completing the exercises, test your AQ again to see how much your responses have changed.

I. Developing Assertive Behaviors

*"There is so much more to be gained from
life by being free and able to stand up for
oneself, and from honoring the same right
for others."*
Robert E. Alberti and Michael L. Emmons
Your Perfect Right

Your development of assertive behavior begins with a few
simple, key concepts. Generally there are three basic ways for people
to act in any given situation: passive, aggressive, and assertive.
These are explained thoroughly in *Your Perfect Right* by Drs. Robert
E. Alberti and Michael L. Emmons. As these three ways of behaving
are described, you will probably find yourself identifying with each
of them as you remember different situations you have experienced
in your life. Since human behavior is complicated and varies from
situation to situation, it is not uncommon for a woman, or any
person for that matter, to find herself being assertive in some
situations, passive at other times, and also occasionally aggressive.
For example, a woman may find it easy to assert herself with a
door-to-door salesperson, yet become quite passive in discussing
money matters with her mate. Furthermore, she may also become
aggressive with her children and overreact with them after being
frustrated for not being assertive in some other situation. Frequently
a woman who is passive will overreact and behave aggressively in
her attempts at being assertive. This overcompensation is common,
especially in one's initial attempts to become assertive. It appears
that the pendulum often must swing to the opposite extreme before
arriving at an equilibrium.

We have added to the three general classifications of behavior given by Alberti and Emmons by treating aggressive behavior in two parts: direct aggression and indirect aggression. We feel that this further distinction is necessary because women more frequently attempt to hide or mask their aggressiveness by being indirect. Being indirect has been a culturally-approved choice for women, while being directly aggressive has been commonly labeled as a very masculine behavior. Other authors have chosen to refer to indirect aggression as covert aggression or passive-aggressive behavior. We chose not to use "covert" since the word has an almost insidious connotation that may make women appear to have preconceived, evil intentions. We do not feel this is true, but that, in fact, women have been given little opportunity to behave in a more direct way. Thus, the fault lies in the conditioning process—*not* within the individual woman. When one is oppressed, one learns to be subtle. Nor do we wish to use the term "passive-aggressive," because it emphasizes a Freudian concept and again could give an inaccurate image of the behavior we are describing.

Perhaps you may have wanted to read this book in order to learn how to act differently in some situations where you feel trapped by your own habit patterns. As the various ways of behaving are presented, it would be helpful for you to imagine which way(s) seem most suited to you and which way(s) you see as difficult alternatives for yourself. It is fairly common for most women to identify with the passive or indirectly aggressive ways of acting rather than the aggressive or assertive. How do you see yourself?

Passive or non-assertive

In the accompanying lifestyles chart, we refer to the passive woman as Doris Doormat. When Doris is being non-assertive, she is typically functioning at a low level. She allows other people to make her decisions for her, even though she may later resent them for it. She feels helpless, powerless, and inhibited. Nervousness and anxiety are not uncommon to Doris. She rarely expresses her feelings and has little self-confidence. She does best when following others and may be fearful of taking the initiative in any situation. Frequently she feels sorry for herself to the point of martyrdom and wonders

SELECTED TYPICAL CHARACTERISTICS	DORIS DOORMAT	AGATHA AGGRESSIVE	IRIS INDIRECT	APRIL ASSERTIVE
Point of view	I'm not OK	You're not OK	You're not OK, but I'll let you think you are	I'm OK and you're OK
Dominant role	inhibited underdog	underdog in bear suit	mad dog in lamb's suit	top-dog
Sample games	"If it weren't for you," "Kick me" and "Why does it always happen to me?"	"Now I've got you!"	"I'm smiling while stabbing you in the back"	"Let's play tennis"
Self-sufficiency	low	high or low	looks high but is usually low	usually high
Decision-making	others choose for her	chooses for others and they know it	chooses for others and they don't know it	chooses for herself
Significant other	Agatha, Iris, or April	Doris	Agatha, April, and/or Doris	herself
Feedback she gets from others	guilt, anger, frustration, disrespect	hurt, defensive, humiliated	confusion, frustration, feels manipulated	you respect me and I respect you
Social pattern	puts herself down	puts herself up by putting others down	appears to put others up while putting them down	puts herself up
Defensive pattern	flees or gives in	outright attack	concealed attack	evaluates and acts
Action pattern	under-reacts	over-reacts	acts indirectly	acts directly
Success pattern	lucks out	beats out others	wins by manipulating others	wins honestly
Potential for	suicide, alcoholism, drug abuse, other withdrawals	committing crimes, homicide	being murdered, provoking retaliation	peaceful, active life

The idea for this chart was modified and adapted from the "Characterological Lifechart of Three Fellows We All Know," by Gerald Piaget presented at the Institute on Assertive Communication, American Orthopsychiatric Association Convention, San Francisco, April, 1974.

why others cannot rescue her from her plight. When a woman has *only* passivity as her style of relating to the world, and she has failed in turning to others, she frequently turns to alcoholism, drugs, physical complaints, or suicide to escape her misery.

Aggressive

On the other hand, the aggressive woman, Agatha Aggressive, is very expressive—mostly to the extent that she humiliates and depreciates the person with whom she is relating. You could call her obnoxious, vicious, or egocentric. No matter what you label her, she has the same destructive effect on you; you feel devastated by an encounter with her. Her message to you is that she's OK and you definitely are not OK. In our society one might say it takes a lot of courage for a woman to be aggressive, especially since this style of behavior has been viewed as totally non-feminine. So, the price the aggressive woman has paid is usually alienation from almost everybody. What a heavy price for anybody to pay just to get what they want!

Indirectly aggressive

Because of the reaction accorded to the aggressive woman and the misery experienced by the passive woman, many women develop the ability to get what they want by indirect means. In our chart Iris Indirect illustrates this style of behavior. Iris has learned her lesson well; in order to achieve he goal she may use trickery, seduction, or manipulation. She sees indirectness as an avenue open to her because society includes this trait in its definition of woman. A woman is expected to use her "womanly wiles" to get what she wants. Therefore, at times Iris is seen as "cute and coy." However, when she is angry, she is likely to use sneaky ways to get revenge. She can be so indirect that the person with whom she is angry may never even know that she was angry or what her anger was about. Iris and many like her enjoy these games that keep her fighting spirit enough so that she doesn't succumb to the depressions of Doris.

Assertive

Many women have been unaware that there is another alternative way of responding to people and situations, i.e., assertively. An assertive action is an alternative to passive or aggressive actions. In our chart, April Assertive, like Agatha, is expressive with her feelings, but not to the point of obnoxiousness. She is able to state her views and desires directly, spontaneously, and honestly. She feels good about herself and about others too; she respects the feelings and rights of other people. April can evaluate a situation, decide how to act, and then act without reservation. The most important thing to April is that she is true to herself. Winning or losing seem unimportant compared to the value of expressing herself and choosing for herself. She may not always achieve her goals, but to her the end-product isn't always as meaningful as the actual process of asserting herself. Regardless of whether April has something positive or negative to say to you, she says it in such a way that you are left with your dignity intact and with good feelings about what was said.

In our classes and workshops women have frequently asked: "Can I be assertive and still be feminine, too?"

Because this is such a popular concern, we give special attention to talking about "feminine assertiveness," which simply means that a woman may incorporate her new assertive skills comfortably into her own style of being a woman. She may *choose* to retain some former ways of acting, speaking, or dressing, which would still fall under the traditional concept of feminity. As long as she is doing this by choice, rather than by mere conformity to society's definition of feminity, we feel that she is being assertive. To choose for oneself is to be assertive.

The following list exemplifies assertive choices that may also be labeled feminine:
- Choosing to cook and do housework at times.
- Choosing to shave her legs because she likes the way they feel to her.
- Choosing to wear a dress instead of pants when others may be in pants.
- Choosing to go into a "female profession," such as teaching, nursing, social work because this really does appeal to her more

than a business career, being a doctor, or becoming an attorney.

• Choosing to remain soft-spoken instead of trying to develop a tougher voice tone than is necessary to be heard.

• Choosing to wear some make-up without feeling inferior if she doesn't "have my face on."

• Choosing to allow someone to open a door for her or to carry something heavy.

• Choosing to be compassionate and nurturing without feeling obligated to do so.

The assertive woman feels free to make any of these choices, even though she may be put down by others for "copping out." *Having to* conform to feminist standards can be just as oppressive as having to conform to the narrow old standards for women. So, let's keep our options alive!

Situational Examples

How each woman responds to given situations tells a lot about her behavior patterns. Examine these situations and find yourself.

What's for Dinner?

Situation: A man and a woman, each with a full-time job, are living together. The woman has her share of housework and cooking, and the man has his share of the domestic chores. She returns from work one evening quite tired to find her mate in the study reading the paper.

Passive (non-assertive): Doris sighs as she enters the study. She felt like going out to dinner and is really too tired to cook dinner by herself, but doesn't say this. She "puts a smile on her face" and asks sweetly, "What would you like for dinner, honey?" She quietly goes off and fixes dinner, feeling all the while like a martyr. Her mother phones while she's preparing dinner, and Doris complains bitterly to her mother that she has to do *all* the work.

Aggressive: Agatha immediately starts moaning about what a hard day she's had. She yells at her mate. If he thinks she's going to cook when she feels this rotten, he's crazy, she screams. She threatens to leave him if he doesn't do something about the messy house and at least take her out to a nice restaurant for dinner. She calls him a "lazy slob" and belittles him for not caring about her feelings. He a) offers to help, b) promises to take her out, or c) goes out, slamming the door behind him.

Indirect Aggression: Iris steps lightly into the study and asks, "What would you like to do about dinner?" She would like him to suggest going out or at least helping, but he's candid and says he's tired and would she mind fixing dinner tonight. Iris makes an attempt to look even more tired and bedraggled, hoping again that he will take the hint. He doesn't. So, she agrees to fix dinner and proceeds to the kitchen, banging pots and pans furiously, preparing something she knows he hates, and burning it besides.

Assertive: April finds her mate in the study and asks that they talk for a minute about plans for dinner. She asks him how he's feeling and proceeds to tell him that she has had a hard day and is feeling quite tired. She suggests that they either fix dinner together or go out to eat, since he said he was feeling tired too. She is empathetic with his feelings, but at the same time does not cheat herself by hiding her own feelings. They reach a compromise and neither one of them feels like a martyr or feels put down. They enjoy dinner together in a relaxed atmosphere.

"How about a little credit?"

Situation: A woman, recently divorced, is on her own and faced with the problem of establishing credit for herself and obtaining some charge cards in her own name. She worked at a less than glamorous job for a few years paying all the bills (which were in her husband's name) while putting her husband through college. Her bank refuses to issue her a charge-all card, since she has no other credit references. She goes into a large department store where she has done business for years as Mrs._____.

Passive (non-assertive): Doris approaches the credit office, fills out an application and waits her turn. She feels anxious and isn't quite sure that she has the right to ask for credit, but everyone has told her this is the way to go about making a new life for herself as an independent woman. She's nervous. She finally speaks to the credit clerk telling her that she would like a new credit card in her own name. The clerk asks why her old card won't do? Doris explains that she's now on her own since her divorce and needs to establish her own credit. The clerk looks at the financial forms Doris has filled out. She tells Doris that since she has *no* credit background of her own, she will be judged by her ex-husband's credit background. She advises Doris to get her own checking account at the bank, so that after a year she'd probably be eligible for a check guarantee and bank credit card. Doris feels quite overwhelmed and says thank you and leaves without pursuing the issue further.

Aggressive: Agatha makes impatient noises until her turn to talk with the credit clerk. She presents the necessary forms, but upon hearing the clerk's explanation she loudly protests that she will have nothing to do with linking her credit potential with that "rotten bum" she was married to. She demands that she be issued credit immediately or she will see to it that she and all of her friends will never shop at this store again. The clerk gets the manager with whom Agatha is very obnoxious. The manager stalls for time and finds a way to avoid Agatha, or turn her down by phone.

Indirect Aggression: Iris walks up to the credit clerk as if she knows what's happening. She proceeds to tell a long, rather confusing story about how desperately she needs a credit card in her own name. Her whole world will cave in without it. She tries her best to elicit the clerk's sympathies, while simultaneously flattering her for being so understanding and helpful (before the clerk has had a chance to be either). She drops the name of the president of the department store as a best friend of hers and tries to manipulate her way out of having to fill out the papers. She insists she doesn't have the time for this, but assures the clerk that she has sound credit elsewhere and is well known and respected about town. The clerk retreats to her supervisor in dismay and frustration.

Assertive: April gives her financial information to the credit clerk stating pleasantly that she would like a card issued in her name as soon as possible. When the clerk explains that this may be difficult, April is not overwhelmed; she again reiterates that it is very important for her to get a credit card and that she would be happy to furnish additional references to expedite the process. She states that she now has a checking account in her own name and her employer would be happy to provide a reference for her. The clerk realizes that April is standing her ground. She consults with her supervisor. April assures the supervisor that with additional references which she will provide, she will definitely qualify for a credit card. April also emphasizes that she has been a good customer of the store for years and intends to continue dealing with them. The supervisor feels that April is sincere and respects her straight forwardness and confidence. She decides to accept April's application.

"You're not interested in my work!"

Situation: A young couple are living together. They are both struggling to achieve success and security in similarly related fields of work. The man begins to complain that the woman is not interested in *his* work because she doesn't take an active and enthusiastic role in finding out more about what he does and why he does it. She isn't usually available to accompany him on business-related trips. He feels she should make a greater effort to be gracious and to entertain his work associates.

Passive (non-assertive): Doris reacts with feelings of guilt. She remembers her traditional upbringing and cliches like—"Stand by your man." Doris is convinced that her partner's success or failure depends a great deal on how much responsibility she takes in playing an auxiliary role in his job. Apologetically she vows to find a way to please him. She represses her own needs regarding *her* work and its limitations and demands. To keep peace, she gives in to his complaints and puts his interests first.

Aggressive: Instantly Agatha's defenses flare up. She begins to argue with her mate, recounting instances when she has supported him and he hasn't appreciated it. Then she launches an attack on him about the times when she needed him, and he obviously didn't care at all. Consequently, they both feel alienated, misunderstood and hurt. The problem is sure to flare up again.

Indirect Aggression: The last thing Iris wants to do is take any responsibility for her partner's accusations. Even if she were guilty of sabotaging his work (which is typical for Iris), she would never admit it. She tries to manipulate her partner by bemoaning how her work "forces" her to be less supportive of him. She is dishonest about "feeling terrible" for him and in her own sweet but back-stabbing way, she puts him down for being "weak" and unable to stand on his own "like a man." She doesn't seem to recognize she would feel differently if the tables were reversed and she needed his support. She feels self-righteous; he feels threatened and alone.

Assertive: In a non-defensive way April listens to her mate's complaints. She encourages him to express all that he is feeling about the situation: his anger, frustration, hurt, aloneness, etc. Then she shares with him how she really feels about the issue. She is able to empathize with his need for support and recognizes the legitimacy of that need within him as well as within herself. April then asserts that there may be some things that each can do to be mutually supportive of the other. She explores the alternatives with him, for example, by suggesting that they spend an hour or a day at each other's place of work once in a while, that they set aside a certain time every day (perhaps after dinner) to talk together about their feelings, that together they plan some social occasions with each other's work associates, etc. They both feel better due to April's assertiveness.

In this chapter we have presented the major ways of behaving in any situation—passive, aggressive and indirectly aggressive, and assertive. By discovering how you behave in your own life, you will be able to recognize situations you could handle more assertively.

As Alberti and Emmons point out in *Your Perfect Right*, non-assertiveness may be *situational* or *generalized*. The same may be true of each of the other types of behavior we have illustrated. You can recall many situations from your personal experience which will correspond to one of the four types of behavior we describe— examine the chart to see which life style is most like your own.

There are many common experiences that will bring out the Doris, Agatha, Iris or April in you. Carefully examine your inter-relationships with other people close to you: your spouse, room-mate, friends, children, parents, brothers or sisters, employer or employees, neighbors, co-workers, teachers, and others. Who is dominant in these specific relationships?

This self-examination is an important step toward identifying your own life style and then setting out to do something about it. Although we recognize that your body and your mind work together, we suggest that you follow this analysis with two separate approaches to becoming assertive: awareness of your body's image and consciousness of your mind's patterns.

II. Your Body—
Developing an Assertive Body Image

"The great thing in the world is not so much where we are but in what direction we are going."
—Oliver Wendell Holmes

Besides knowing the right words to say, many times the assertive woman will find that how she acts and how she says something has an even greater impact than what she says. For this reason, she needs to consider ways of assertive body image and style.

Sharon Bower, in her manual, *Learning Assertive Behavior With PALS*, (Stanford University), speaks to women about learning how to develop an assertive appearance by taking each component of behavior and focusing on each action separately.

Numerous research studies (Wolpe & Lazarus, 1969; Serber, 1972; Miller, and Hersen, 1973; Hersen, Eisler, & Miller, 1973) stress the importance of the non-verbal components of assertive behavior. Entire books have also been written dealing exclusively with non-verbal behaviors, such as *Body Language* and *Non-Verbal Communication*.

Your body does communicate. Your style of emotional expression, posture, facial expressions, and voice quality are all tremendously important to you in becoming an assertive woman. This chapter will help you to develop an assertive body image to make your body, as well as your words, communicate assertively.

An inventory of body image components

The process of self-analysis is a simple one. Methodically check yourself from head to toe, as you probably do frequently during the day, but this time measure yourself on a scale of assertiveness.

For example, women often have a problem making *eye contact* with another person because many of us have been taught that it is more feminine to look away or look down. At times it is considered coy to give little side glances and not to look directly at someone for any length of time. In some ethnic cultures, it is considered disrespectful for women to make direct eye contact with men or authority figures. However, in our society making eye contact and holding your head erect is essential when you want to appear assertive and interested. This does not require staring at someone; look into their eyes, then perhaps look away for a few seconds or drop your gaze slightly so that you are focusing on their mouth as they speak to you. Practice making good eye contact with someone as you are talking and be aware of any differences in the quality of your communication. Are you listening better? Are you conveying more interest and receiving more interest in what you are saying?

What do your *facial expressions* say about you? Many women find it easy to smile and to demonstrate warmth, but when it comes to expressing anger or disapproval, they may do so with a smile on their face. Thus, the woman's smile looks like a nervous tic and she gives a double message when she smiles, yet says that she is very angry. Look in a mirror and see how you look when you are expressing anger, joy, sadness, fear, and other emotions. Get feedback from your friends, too. Practice making your face and head look assertive: make direct eye contact, feel the control over your facial muscles, and hold your head high.

While you are looking in the mirror, check out your *posture*. Changing your posture can change the way you feel about yourself. Try assuming a passive stance. Then change to an assertive stance— lean slightly forward with feet solidly grounded. Enjoy feeling centered with your body. Learn how close you like to stand or sit next to another person. This is your "optimal distance." To find your *optimal distance*, stand across the room from a friend, face each other, and walk slowly toward your friend as she remains stationary. Make eye contact with her the whole way and then stop walking as soon as you feel that you are at a comfortable distance from her. Measure this distance, and then have your friend repeat the process. You will discover that each person has her own optimal distance that aids assertion. If you can be aware of this fact with other people, it will help you to maintain an assertive posture. Assertiveness allows you to move toward a person, while passiveness involves hesitation, or moving away.

Next on your checklist for an assertive body image, notice your *hand and arm gestures*. Do people say that you could not talk if someone tied your hands behind your back? If so, this means that your gestures are so distracting that they may prevent you from delivering an assertive message. On the other hand, if you hold your arms rigid against your body or fold them across your chest, you create a passive image. Being able to move your hands and arms about in an expansive way demonstrates a sense of confidence and freedom. There are two kinds of gestures you should practice. *Descriptive gestures* are those in which you practically "paint a picture in the sky" by sketching a scene or object in the air. Try this while describing your house to someone. The other type of gestures are *emphatic*. These emphasize the significance of what you are saying, e.g. shaking your fist to show anger or pounding on a table to get someone's attention or putting your hand on someone's shoulder to connote caring and concern. Practice using emphatic gestures to show positive, as well as negative feelings.

How are you dressed today? What sort of image do you convey by your *style of dress*? It is common knowledge that dressing appropriately for a job interview can increase your chances of getting the job. But do you realize that you can dress assertively too? Dressing in a favorite outfit can give you that extra touch of confidence to help you be assertive. Whenever you are feeling down, you can be assertive with yourself by wearing an outfit that doesn't let you "fade into the woodwork," but attracts attention and helps you to project an outgoing appearance without being "loud" or "coarse." Of course, these styles vary with each individual. So, check out your own particular wardrobe and decide what your most assertive outfits are and use them as allies to help you.

The topic of dress styles relates to the whole area of personal grooming and a healthful appearance. While we do not choose to recommend specific books or methods for diet, exercise or personal health, we recognize that your increased self-awareness will be accompanied by changes in these areas of your life.

There may be some special concerns you have about developing an assertive body image.

For example, some overweight women in our workshops admit to us that they have used their weight as a way to remain passive sexually or to avoid sexual encounters altogether. Similarly, women who have felt self-conscious about skin problems such as acne tend to be withdrawn and passive individuals. Even when such conditions no longer persist, many women continue to see themselves as "overweight" or "acne-prone." In any case, practicing more assertive behaviors and working to develop a more assertive attitude can do much more than losing extra weight or visiting a dermatologist can do alone.

Probably one of the most vital body tools you can develop in becoming assertive is your *voice*. If you have a tape recorder or a friend to listen and give feedback, try to evaluate your voice in several different ways. Women, for the most part, seem to have higher-pitched but softer voices than men. However, for some, this is a conditioned tone rather than our natural voice. In many instances Doris has tried to sound like a "baby doll" by raising the pitch of her voice, or Iris has considered it feminine and sexy to "purr like a kitten." Unfortunately, these tones do not sound sincere, straight forward, or assertive, but are obvious distortions of what is natural. A lower-pitched voice is more often associated with assertion. Try to recite a poem in which you alternate raising and lowering your pitch to get a feeling for how you can vary and control your voice. Variations in pitch reflect emotional feelings. This is another quality that women have been conditioned to adopt. Overdoing it may make you sound like a comedian or appear hysterical or seem to be out of control. On the other hand, if you use almost no variation of pitch you risk being a boring speaker or sounding impersonal.

When analyzing your voice try to gauge the *volume* of it. Are you afraid to speak up for fear you will sound masculine? A woman can be loud and clear and still sound like a woman. It is better to be heard than to be disregarded. And yet, like Agatha, if you speak very loudly most of the time, you will risk turning people off.

Many times women give away the fact that they are nervous or anxious by speaking too rapidly. Your *rate of speech* needs to be evenly paced, not too fast or slow. Sometimes a slower rate is good in order to emphasize an important idea. Again, when angry, a woman may tend to talk very fast, trying to get it all said before she "runs out of steam." This is not necessary. You can command someone's attention for a long time if you remember to use good eye contact and the other body elements we have mentioned. Also, *stressing* important words (usually nouns and verbs) can help you to sound assertive. Try emphasizing important words in a sentence, sometimes pausing before or after the word, by speaking key words louder, or by enunciating slowly and precisely.

Finally you should be aware of the *quality* of your voice. Do you tend to whine when feeling helpless, powerless, or manipulative? Or, when nervous, does your voice become raspy and harsh? Practice asking for favors without whining. Try saying things that you are normally uncomfortable in saying, without a harsh, rasping tone. Most people will listen and respect a full-bodied voice tone rather than a squeaky, strident one.

How you say something rather than *what* you say can be most effective. You do not need a college education or a big vocabulary to be assertive and make yourself heard. If you practice the behaviors we have described and keep your messages simple, direct, and spontaneous, you will be on the way to becoming an assertive woman. In later chapters, we will focus on specific techniques to deal with particular situations where the content of what you say can make a big difference.

The assertive woman will try to develop style and body image that April projects. She uses good eye contact. Her face is expressive and her expressions match the content of what she is saying. She's aware of her posture and projects an assertive stance. Through the use of appropriate hand and arm gestures she creates a feeling of expansiveness in her audience. Her style of dress adds to her confidence. April also uses her voice as an ally. She has control over her tone, volume, rate, and quality; she uses appropriate inflections and is careful to stress important words when she's making a special point. Most of all, April puts herself up confidently by developing her assertive style instead of faltering over the right words to say. In fact, April can probably deliver her sentence half-backwards and still sound good.

Reducing anxiety and promoting relaxation

The assertive woman not only knows how to develop her body image, she knows how to promote her own physical well-being. There are many sources of information on healthful food habits and exercise. We assume these are available to you. Our concern is with more subtle body influences, especially nervousness and anxiety, which afflict many women.

Anxiety will detract from your assertive body image because it shows itself in your behavior. For most people, acting assertively in new situations evokes some initial anxiety and nervousness, which can be alleviated by acting and by learning to relax.

What happens to your body when you feel anxious? Headaches, a "nervous stomach," asthma, and "dizzy spells" are common bodily indicators of anxiety. In more extreme forms, anxiety can be severe enough to be a contributing factor to ulcers, migraine headaches and heart attacks. In addition to the physical discomfort anxiety can produce, it can also cause emotional discomfort. Some people get "cold feet" and so avoid approaching employers for a raise in salary and forego the additional income; "stage fright" prevents many people from speaking in front of a group, even though the speech may have been interesting and valuable to the group; others "clam up" when they are treated unfairly and sacrifice their self respect in the process.

When facing threatening and anxiety provoking situations, Doris Doormat feels she has *no control* over her anxiety. Her anxiety immobilizes and controls her. Being passive, Doris is frequently anxious and frustrated. Her anxiety is often at such a high level that she suffers from severe headaches or from fainting spells.

She avoids anxiety-provoking situations because she feels powerless to do anything about them. The more she tries to avoid anxiety-provoking situations, the stronger her anxiety becomes about facing them. The assertive woman, in contrast, is not a helpless victim of anxiety; she alleviates it by taking action.

By acting and therefore having control over what you do, you make it impossible for anxiety to control you. If you have felt that you couldn't tolerate a threatening situation—that your anxiety is so great that you really couldn't "live through it—you have probably felt helpless to say or do anything. When you know that you can choose to assert yourself, you can live through threatening encounters and alleviate your anxiety because you can *benefit*, physically and/or emotionally, by saying or doing something. The value of this concept is stressed by Bower and others, including Butler, Cotler and Guerra.

Learning to relax can combat anxiety and be a good complement to assertion. You probably already practice forms of relaxation such as meditation, yoga, or a walk on the beach. While relaxation is not *necessary* for effective assertions, it can help you to feel more in control of your body.

You have probably noticed that you feel calmer and more relaxed after you have rested quietly even for a short time. By learning deep muscle relaxation, or any other forms of relaxation, you will be able to relax beyond this usual point. We recommend beginning with deep muscle relaxation as the easiest form to learn, but we also encourage you to explore other forms of relaxation. With practice you will be able to relax at will and counteract the tensions of anxiety arising from threatening situations.

We suggest that you practice deep muscle relaxation twice a day for one week. Try to be aware of particular muscle groups that are more difficult to relax than others, and give them special attention. For many people, the stomach, shoulders, and back are almost constantly tensed. When you have learned how to relax, you can practice relaxation together with acting assertively. Remember that you will alleviate your anxiety most effectively when you *act* as an assertive woman.

Training yourself in deep muscle relaxation

You can use this guide to train yourself in deep muscle relaxation, a technique first developed by Jacobsen in 1938. Choose a quiet, comfortable place where you won't be disturbed for half an hour. Go through relaxation while lying on the floor, a bed, or a reclining chair.

Concentrate on the muscle groups below, one at a time in the order presented. Create tension in the muscles by tightening them for five seconds and then relaxing them. For each muscle group a method is described for creating tension and achieving relaxation The first time you try it, go through the procedure for each muscle group twice.

It is awkward to read the instructions while attempting to relax, and it may be inconvenient to have someone read the instructions to you. We suggest that an ideal method is to use a commercial tape recording of relaxation instructions (see *Bibliography*), or to make your own tape recording.

Muscle	Tensing Method
Forehead	Wrinkle forehead. Try to make your eyebrows touch your hairline for five seconds. Relax.
Eyes and nose	Close your eyes as tightly as you can for five seconds. Relax.
Lips, cheeks, and jaw	Draw corners of your mouth back and grimace for five seconds. Relax. Feel the calmness and warmth in your face.
Hands	Extend arms in front of you, clench fists tightly for five seconds. Relax, and feel the warmth and calmness in your hands.
Forearms	Extend arms out against an invisible wall and push forward with hands for five seconds. Relax.
Upper arms	Bend elbows. Tense biceps for five seconds. Relax, and feel the tension leave your arms.
Shoulders	Shrug shoulders up to your ears for five seconds. Relax.
Back	Arch your back off the floor or bed for five seconds. Relax. Feel the anxiety and tension disappearing.

Stomach	Tighten your stomach muscles for five seconds. Relax.
Hips, buttocks	Tighten buttocks for five seconds. Relax.
Thighs	Tighten thigh muscles by pressing legs together as tightly as you can for five seconds. Relax.
Feet	Bend ankles toward your body as far as you can, for five seconds. Relax.
Toes	Curl toes under as tightly as you can for five seconds. Relax.

Constructing your assertive behavior hierarchy

Dealing with tension and anxiety by relaxation is only a first step, although it is one that should be repeated as often as necessary. Your next step is to gain a better understanding of your sources of anxiety. What particular situations or encounters make you feel anxious? What causes you to be passive and non-assertive, causing you emotional and/or physical harm? What triggers your anger or aggression? It will be helpful for you to identify specific instances in which you would like to be more assertive. You can use the Assertive Behavior Hierarchy to specify situations in which you find it difficult to assert yourself.

The hierarchy has been used by Pamela Butler at the Behavior Therapy Institute in Sausalito, California in her assertive training groups, and we also use it in our workshops. The hierarchies help to identify each member's specific assertive deficits, and group time is spent rehearsing the hierarchy items to minimize anxiety and learn assertive responses.

The hierarchy items are ordered according to the degree of anxiety produced by each situation, beginning with the least anxiety-provoking. Experiencing success with the first hierarchy items will encourage you to continue to practice assertive behaviors and responses as you face more demanding situations as an assertive woman.

Constructing and using your hierarchy will help you to become more aware of the specific times you behave non-assertively. It will also provide you with a starting point for the application of suggestions from this book to your own life.

It is important that you proceed through your hierarchy in order; resist the temptation to jump to the last items of your hierarchy before you feel comfortable with the first ones. When you are comfortable asserting yourself with minor anxiety-provoking items, you'll find it much easier to proceed to the more difficult ones, and so increase the likelihood that you'll become an assertive woman.

Before completing your own hierarchy, study these examples:

Doris Doormat Hierarchy

1. Returning that faulty toaster to the department store.
2. Initiating a conversation with my brother's new partner, Bill.
3. Asking not to be interrupted when Agatha starts talking in middle of my conversation with April.
4. Cutting telephone calls short when I am busy, especially with Iris and Agatha.
5. Asking questions of my car dealer without fear of sounding weak and stupid.
6. Giving a sincere compliment to my spouse or close friend.
7. Telling April when I have done something important or worthwhile.
8. Refusing unreasonable requests from my family, employer, and friends, especially Iris Indirect and Agatha Aggressive.
9. Telling my spouse or close friend or relative that I disagree with their opinion on a subject.
10. Expressing my anger to a very close relative or to my spouse in a non-apologetic way.

Agatha Aggressive Hierarchy

1. Complaining about the poor restaurant service assertively, without name-calling.
2. Not interrupting Doris or April in the middle of their conversation.
3. In my classes, letting Doris and Iris speak up without answering for them.

4. Listening to April criticize me for coming on too strong, without attacking her or being too defensive.
5. Not being overly critical of Doris because I know she won't fight back.
6. Expressing my positive feelings to April, Iris, and Doris, by telling them when I appreciate something they have done.
7. Not bullying or shaming Doris into doing me a favor, knowing she'll be too guilty to say "no."
8. Being aware of another person's faults or vulnerabilities without teasing and making fun of her/him.
9. Talking about differences of opinion with my mate or close friend, not just saying "you're wrong."
10. Expressing anger without hitting, or throwing things, or being accusing or blaming.

Iris Indirect Hierarchy

1. Asking Doris to drive me to work when my car is being repaired, without making her feel guilty if she can't drive me.
2. Give a compliment and approval openly and honestly, and not by using false flattery.
3. Being more direct when refusing door-to-door salespeople; not saying "my husband won't let me buy it," etc.
4. Not making sarcastic or caustic comments about others behind their back.
5. Ask for something specific from my spouse without being dishonest and manipulative about why I want it.
6. When Agatha asks something unreasonable of me, saying "no" directly without becoming sullen and hostile.
7. Initiating the expression of love or affection with my mate without manipulating or being coy.
8. Expressing valid criticisms to my spouse honestly without resorting to indirect put-downs.
9. Asking for love and attention to be given to me without using guilt or manipulations to get it.
10. Expressing my anger openly to Doris, Agatha, or April by honestly stating that I am angry, instead of giving them the "silent treatment."

Your Own Assertive Behavior Hierarchy

Instructions: To construct your own hierarchy select as the first item or situation something you feel you could handle assertively with only minimal anxiety. Continue to order your items from least anxiety-provoking to most anxiety-provoking. The last items should be the behaviors or situations that cause you the greatest anxiety and discomfort.

1. _____

2. _____

3. _____

4. _____

5. _____

6. _____

7. _____

8. _____

9. _____

10. _____

III. Your Mind—
Developing an Assertive Attitude

"The first and great commandment is, don't let them scare you."
—*Elmer Davis*
But We Were Born Free

Because assertion is a very personal, rather than mechanical, learning experience, it is necessary for you first to know yourself so that you can adapt assertion to your own particular needs. Assertion is only one tool that you may choose to employ to better your life. It is not the answer to every question; it is not the solution to every problem. As you explore your attitudes and deepen your awareness you will be better able to identify the ways in which assertion can be valuable to you personally.

Developing an awareness of what is normally accepted as feminine, as well as an awareness of the transition that women are going through today, is part of the "consciousness raising" process experienced by the assertive woman. This process usually occurs in small groups in which women examine traditional values and stereotypes in a very supportive atmosphere which is conducive to helping women to grow and change. Many of these discussions motivate women to action and to attempt to assert themselves.

In Chapter XIII "Women Together", we talk more about the consciousness raising group as a special resource, and mention sources of further information.

Apart from group experiences, a woman can increase her own consciousness raising with such techniques as our "consciousness razors" provided here for your use. The concept of consciousness raising certainly has merit; it describes the process of increasing one's awareness level and heightening one's perceptions. Yet we especially like the pun on the word "razor", because it implies that each razor has a sharp edge to help you cut through some attitudes that may inhibit your assertiveness

Using consciousness razors

Following are a list of razors. Try to answer each item as honestly as possible. After responding to each item, review your comments carefully.

• Have you ever felt different from other women? _____
_____

• Have you felt competitive with other women?_____
_____

• Were you treated differently from your brother(s) as you were growing up? How? _____
_____

• Have you ever felt pressured into having sex? _____
_____

• Have you ever pressured yourself into having sex? _____
_____

• Have you ever lied about orgasm?_____
_____

• Have you ever felt like a sex object? _____
_____

• Do you ever feel invisible? _____
_____

• Do you often feel insignificant? _____
_____

• What was your relationship to your parents? _____
_____

• What was your parents' relationship to you? _____
_____

• How was your education affected by your being female? _____

- How was your interest in sports affected by your being female?

- How was your career choice affected by your being female?

- How do you feel about getting old? _____

- How do you feel about your mother's aging? _____

- What do you fear most about aging?_____

- What goal have you wanted most to achieve in your life? _____

- What, if anything, has stopped you from achieving this goal?

- Do you see yourself operating in a dependent and/or in an independent way? How? _____

- How do you relate to authority figures? (Clergy, doctor, police, etc.) _____

- Have you ever felt powerful? _____

- How do you feel about your body? _____

- Have you ever punished yourself? When? How?_____

- Have you ever forbidden yourself a pleasure, a meal, or some gratification? _____
- Have you ever pinched or slapped yourself? _____

- Do you often feel a sense of aloneness or loneliness? _____

- Do you have some attitudes that could inhibit your being more assertive? _____
- What are they?_____

- Which affect you the most? _____
- Which affect you the least?_____

_____

As you review your comments on the consciousness razors, look for:

• Patterns or habits that seem to repeat themselves over and over in your life.

• Rationalizations about why you do or don't do something instead of expressing your honest feelings.

Explore your feelings in depth, trying to avoid an intellectual exercise in pursuit of the "right" answer. The goal of consciousness raising is to know yourself better and to accept who you are as well as to undertake the changes that you decide to make.

Getting out of The Compassion Trap

We believe that one particular attitude or "trap" prevents women from acting in more assertive ways: The Compassion Trap. We give it special attention here because it affects all women in our society on one or more levels. Your recognition and understanding of the Compassion Trap and how it affects *you* personally is an important part of developing an assertive attitude.

In her article, "The Compassion Trap" (From *Woman in Sexist Society: Studies in Power and Powerlessness*, edited by Vivian Gornick and Barbara Moran, New York, Basic Books, Inc., 1971.) Margaret Adams defines the Compassion Trap as a trap exclusive to women who feel that they exist to serve others, and who believe that thay must provide tenderness and compassion to all at all times. This attitude is very difficult to throw off, but avoiding the Compassion Trap is essential for the assertive women.

Years ago, it was a very important job for Doris to "keep the family together" through her self-sacrificing and compromising, while the man of the house endured many hassles outside the home in the industrial world. Overall, the totally compassionate woman benefitted society by making things comfortable, so that men could tend to the "more important concerns," of work, business, science, and politics. Now, although women have begun to move out of the home, they still tend to cluster toward the "helping professions" (social work, nursing, teaching, domestic services, etc.) in which they may extend their roles in providing care and compassion for those whom they serve. However, many a Doris becomes frustrated and confused as she tries to follow her own individual preferences while still looking out for the needs of others. She is torn between expressing herself directly and thus reaping firsthand rewards, and supporting others, thereby receiving vicarious pleasure from the accomplishments of others.

Because the Compassion Trap dictates that a woman express herself through meeting the needs of others, it frequently prevents a woman from being assertive. The assertive woman feels the freedom to be direct, and to act on her own behalf, while at times she may *choose* to be compassionate. She rarely feels, however, that she *must* always be compassionate to the exclusion of her own feelings. In this area it has been very difficult for some women to burst through traditional barriers. Women often have colluded with each other and reinforced one another for being devoted and dedicated to others, perpetuating the Compassion Trap to the utmost degree. Women in the Compassion Trap place greater importance on taking care of others' feelings than on meeting their own needs.

Getting out of the Compassion Trap does not mean that, like Agatha, you must become insensitive to others' feelings. Instead, it means valuing your own feelings and being responsive to them with the same care that you give to others, as April does.

Generally, we find five areas in which Doris, Agatha, or Iris may find herself in the Compassion Trap:

1. She may see herself in a protective role, as a mother with children who is afraid to act on her own behalf for fear that there will be negative repercussions toward those whom she is trying to protect.

2. A woman who is single may give up career opportunities to take care of her aging or sick relatives.

3. An employed woman may be reluctant to leave an unsatisfactory job for fear that her clients will suffer in the short run, even though she may benefit in the long run.

4. When no one else is concerned about a problem situation, a woman may enjoy being seen as the one who has special understanding or compassion.

5. Whenever a crisis arises, a woman may be willing to push aside a creative project to give her full attention to the crisis; she feels indispensable. Some case stories will illustrate the chief variations of the Compassion Trap:

"I felt sorry for him"

Situation: A young woman in her teens and her boyfriend are alone at a very "romantic" place. They have been getting closer and closer to actually having sexual intercourse, but always stopping just before that. Tonight he has decided will be the night to "go all the way."

Aggressive. Agatha, also being caught in the Compassion Trap, feels that the best way to avoid a confrontation is to attack. She accuses her boyfriend of being a sex maniac, and only having "one thing on his mind all of the time." She feels it is unnecessary to listen to him, because her philosophy is "a good offense is the best defense." She prevents him from expressing his feelings, and continues to overreact. For Agatha, it is embarassing to think that she could be caught in a weak moment of compassion, so she uses her aggressiveness to mask her indecision. Agatha cannot believe that expressing her feelings in an assertive way will have any impact, and she feels that the only way she can get her point across is to come on strong.

Passive. Doris, caught in the Compassion Trap, listens intently to her boyfriend recount the numerous occasions when he felt so frustrated after being with her that he couldn't sleep all night. Doris feels guilty as he describes the actual pain he felt by not being able to ejaculate so many times in a row, night after night. She's far too embarrassed to ask him if he ever thought of masturbating to relieve the pressure. Instead, Doris is swept up in his intense feelings, letting herself forget about her own desire not to have sex. She gives in because she feels she can no longer allow him to suffer, and she is secretly fearful that if she doesn't give in, she'll lose him and maybe nobody else will want her.

Indirect. Iris, like Doris, is not immune to the Compassion Trap. She feels sorry for her boyfriend, but she tries to mask her compassion and her panic by making false excuses. For example, Iris lies about having her period and flowing so heavily that to have intercourse would be "very messy and not much fun." If this excuse does not appear to have the impact on her boyfriend that she intends, she will add more bodily complaints such as having a headache or being too tired. Iris may even pretend to want him passionately while she makes up another story about having to get home early or having made a commitment to her parents or her best friend that she would not indulge in any sexual activities that night. Iris fears that her boyfriend will not accept the truth, but she is convinced he will accept excuses! When he finds out, he gets angry.

Assertive. April listens to her boyfriend's feelings and complaints. She acknowledges how miserable he is feeling. She says, however, that in all honesty she does not want to "go all the way" at this time. When he accuses her of being unfair and leading him on, she again repeats that it is very important to her at this time not to have sex, that she respects his feelings, and that perhaps they need to talk about alternatives such as masturbation, avoiding heavy "make-out" sessions, or not seeing each other. She expresses her concern for her own feelings without feeling guilty or compelled to take care of his needs. She feels confident that, if he decides not to see her anymore, she can find someone else who will be willing to respect her wishes.

In this situation April may be refusing to go along with what her boyfriend wants for legitimate reasons that may be religious, political, or very personal in nature. For example, April may have been brought up with the religious belief that she must remain a virgin until she marries. Or April may be a militant feminist who believes that the best way to have political impact is not to engage in sexual intercourse with men. Again, April may be refusing her boyfriend's request because she has a health problem that may make intercourse painful for her. Whatever her real reasons, April may choose to offer such a legitimate reason without feeling that she is making excuses.

From this situation alone, we hope it is clear that it does not require a special background or unique type of woman to become an Assertive April. Many different types of people can be assertive, like April, each in her/his own personal way, and within the context of the special nature of her/his own life situation.

"They need me—the poor things"

Situation: A married woman, who is a competent, experienced nurse, is employed in a hospital with a low salary and poor working conditions. Her income is not vital to the family's welfare; she is working primarily because of her need for self-fulfillment. However, she is confronted with a disorganized hospital administration reflected by under-staffing, inadequate procedures and supplies, and low morale among the nursing staff. A union organizer is trying to unite the nurses to take a stand and, if necessary, to strike for better conditions.

Passive. Caught in the Compassion Trap, Doris believes that she and the other nurses would only be selfish to engage in hard-nosed negotiations that may lead to a strike. After all, who would see to it that Ms. Jones down the hall really swallowed her medication instead of hiding it under her tongue? Doris decides to put up with the poor conditions "for the sake of" her patients. Besides, she's frightened of confrontations and believes that a "good nurse" has to think of others first, keep peace and keep smiling.

Indirect Aggression. Iris feels very helpless when she's caught in the Compassion Trap. She is feeling sorry for her patients, for herself, and for the other nurses. However, her inability to directly express her frustration leads her to fault finding with other nurses, neglecting of her patients, and developing a "who cares?" attitude.

Aggressive. Agatha is also caught in the Compassion Trap and though she feels her intentions are honorable, she is unable to communicate her concern. Instead she gives the impression that she is just an "angry bitch." Taking action seems to be Agatha's only way of coping with this situation. But, as usual, she over-reacts by making hostile demands and threats. She goes to the right people at the top, but she says all of the wrong things. The net result is that she widens the gap of misunderstanding.

Assertive. Like Agatha, April believes in the value of taking action. She is concerned about her patients' welfare, but she chooses to take the risk of a possible strike in order to obtain better conditions for all in the long run. She is confident that the nurses, if united, can make a substantial impact on changing the poor conditions in the hospital. April puts her compassion to good use and doesn't allow her energies to dissipate in a flurry of worry. She expresses her concern to the other nurses and urges them to organize and to take a strong, but fair, stand.

On a practical level it is important for us as women to look at the consequences of what we do. April asks: are we *really* helping other people so much by always pampering them and taking care of things that cause them discomfort? What price do *we* pay as individuals when our giving and compassion is done at the expense of our own happiness? What price does the *receiver* of our compassion pay when we have felt obligated and resentful? Many times, just as much or more can be accomplished if we allow others to be assertive and take responsibility for themselves, while we pursue what is best for us. Whenever you are assertive, you make it possible for yourself to grow and change without cramping anybody else's style. Consider the implications of both men and women taking turns playing the compassionate role. Nothing is a trap as long as you know that you will exercise your right to do or not to do according to what feels best for you.

The Compassion Trap Quiz

Gauge the extent to which you are in the Compassion Trap by taking our quiz below. Answer each question *honestly*. If you have not personally experienced some situations, choose the response that most closely approximates the way you think you would respond. After you have finished, turn the page and add up your score. The corresponding key will help you to determine how "trapped" you really are.

1. You have been seeing this man socially for several weeks, but you are beginning to feel bored and disinterested in continuing the relationship. He likes you very much and would like to see you more often. Do you:

    a) tell him you'd prefer not to see him, feeling you've been honest with yourself?

    b) feel a sudden attack of the Hong-Kong flu coming on?

    c) continue to be the object of his affections, because leaving would really hurt his ego?

    d) tell him that he bores you to tears, and that even if you were both marooned on a desert island, you would camp out on the opposite shore?

2. You invited a friend of yours who lives out of the state to spend her/his two week vacation with you at your home. It is now one month later, and your friend shows no intention of leaving, or reimbursing you for food and telephone bills. You would like your friend to leave. Do you:

    a) not mention anything about your expenses or feelings, because you don't want to damage the friendship?

    b) leave a note saying that you're terribly sorry, but your mother has decided to live with you and you'll need the room?

    c) tell your friend that you really value your friendship, and that her/his extended visit is putting a strain on it. You ask that your friend make plans to leave?

    d) put all of your friend's belongings out on the doorstep with a note: "Don't call me; I'll call you?"

3. You are enjoying one of your rare visits to San Francisco, and you are staying with your brother and sister-in-law. One of your favorite

things to do in San Francisco is to sample the fine restaurants. Your brother and sister-in-law are terrible cooks, but they insist on "treating" you by cooking for you themselves. You would much prefer going out to eat. Do you:

a) decide to have dinner at your brother and sister-in-law's home because you don't want to disappoint them by refusing their offer?

b) tell them that you appreciate their thoughtfulness, and explain that one of the reasons you come to San Francisco is to enjoy the restaurants? You suggest that all of you go out to eat instead.

c) loudly tell them that you're not there for *their* food?

d) call and claim that you are unavoidably detained, and tell them not to wait dinner for you—then sneak out and eat by yourself?

4. You are working on a project that is very important to you. Some friends drop by unexpectedly. You'd really like to continue working on your project. Do You:

a) shelve your project, prepare hors d'oeuvres, and apologize for your cluttered living room?

b) loudly berate your friends for not having called first?

c) explain that you're in the middle of an important project and arrange to see them at a mutually convenient time?

d) ignore your friends and continue working on your project while they are there, hoping they'll get the message.

5. Your ten-year-old daughter customarily walks to school, but today she wants you to drive her. You have driven her on rainy days, but it is not raining today. She continues to ask you to drive her, adding, "Besides, everyone else's mothers drive them." Do you:

a) tell your daughter she can walk to school today, as usual?

b) begin by telling your daughter that you won't drive her to school but after a short time you give in and drive her, feeling guilty that you hesitated?

c) reply "Oh, okay, I'll drive you," thinking of all the other children whose mothers faithfully drive them? You will feel like a neglectful mother if you don't drive your daughter to school?

d) threaten to call the truant officer and report on your daughter if she doesn't leave for school immediately?

Key

1. a) An assertive choice. (3)
   b) Honesty is the best policy here. (0)
   c) Don't forget *your* feelings. (0)
   d) Don't forget *his* feelings. (0)
2. a) You'll feel resentful later. You're trapped. (0)
   b) This may get her/him out, but how do you feel
      about trapping yourself with *that* one? (1)
   c) Right. This will also get her/him out, and
      leave you with your self-respect. (3)
   d) This will get your friend out of your life, also. (0)
3. a) This Compassion Trap will result in your
      disappointment and indigestion. (0)
   b) The assertive thing to do. (3)
   c) Better look for a hotel room—your brother
      and sister-in-law won't want to have you
      as a guest for some time. (0)
   d) You'll soon run out of excuses. Then what? (0)
4. a) The Compassion Trap. (0)
   b) Only if you *never* want to see them again. (0)
   c) Ain't it the truth? (3)
   d) You're wasting time; it may take hours for them
      to get the hint! (0)
5. a) You've got it! (3)
   b) A good start—but you're in the Compassion
      Trap here. (1)
   c) Are you really neglectful? The Compassion
      Trap again. (0)
   d) You avoided the Compassion Trap, but stepped
      into the Aggression Trap! (0)

Add up your total points and gauge the extent of *your* Compassion Trap:

14+: We couldn't ask for more. You can choose what to do without being trapped. Be on the lookout, though, for other situations that may trap you.

9-13: You can avoid the Compassion Trap most of the time, and you're moving in the right direction. Give some extra attention to the people/situations that continue to trap you, and attempt more assertive ways of handling them.

2-8: Consider the price you are paying when you do things at the expense of your own happiness. With some practice, you *can* leave the Compassion Trap and *enjoy* what you *choose* to do. Be an assertive woman and be loved for it.

Choosing your own labels

Developing an assertive attitude is an important part of becoming an assertive woman. If your attitudes and feelings about being assertive are positive and supportive, you can *reward* your assertive behavior. However, if you feel you are being "impolite," "bossy," or "bitchy" when you assert yourself, you can inhibit your assertive behavior and seriously weaken your assertive attitude. You can strengthen or minimize your assertive skills by the *labels* you place on them.

Do the labels *you* apply to your assertive behavior encourage or prevent you from being assertive? Use *positive* self-labels to support and encourage your assertive behavior. ("I'm really being assertive— I love it") *Negative* self-labels can only serve to inhibit and prevent your assertiveness. ("What a bitch I am!")

Other people can mislabel your assertive behavior also. Because women have been expected to behave passively for so long, becoming an assertive woman seems to be an extreme contrast. Other people's expectations of how you behave are being thwarted if you have been consistently passive with them, and are now being assertive. They will be quick to label your behavior as aggressive in an attempt to inhibit it, fearing they may have to change, too. This is particularly true for people close to you (family members, other relatives, close friends, employers) who have in some way benefited from your passivity, as with the Compassion Trap. On the other hand, if you have been consistently aggressive in your interactions with others, moving to a more assertive way of relating will usually be encouraged, and given positive labels by those around you.

Be aware of the negative self-labels you attach to your assertive behavior, and work toward replacing those labels with more positive ones. If you do this, other people can follow your example and work at changing their labels also. Use the following exercise to see how *you* label your assertive behavior by comparing your responses with the responses of our four women, Doris Doormat, Agatha Aggressive, Iris Indirect, and April Assertive. Each of these situations were handled assertively, but it is the label each woman has attached to the assertive behavior that varies here. How would you label each assertion?

"Thanks, but no thanks . . ."

You have been telephoned by a solicitor who is trying to sell you a magazine subscription. You say you aren't interested in receiving the magazine and end the conversation. Do you think to yourself:

Doris Doormat: I really didn't *want* the magazine, but wasn't I impolite and irritable to say so? The next time I'm asked to subscribe, I'll be more polite and do it.

Iris Indirect: Well, I certainly was easy on him! I should have said yes, and then refused to pay the subscription to teach them a lesson about bothering me.

Agatha Aggressive: I wish I'd given that solicitor a piece of my mind! What an insolent person! The next time that happens I won't be so mild-mannered and meek.

April Assertive: I was really assertive with that solicitor. I feel good about being honest and direct, and I didn't fall into the Compassion Trap.

"Get ready for dinner"

Your children are playing outside and you want them to come in for dinner. You go outside and tell them it's time for dinner and to come in now. They protest that it's not that late and couldn't they play for a while longer? You firmly tell them again to come in, and they do. Do you think to yourself:

Doris Doormat: I'm glad they came in, but wasn't I nagging and bossy? I don't want to nag, so I think in the future I'll ask once, and if they don't come in, I'll just try to keep dinner warm.

Iris Indirect: I'm sure they would have come in sooner if I'd not been so polite. Instead of asking twice, I should have just said okay and waited until dinner was burned for them to come in. Then they'd feel bad.

Agatha Aggressive: Was I quiet and passive! What a softie! Next time I'll teach those kids who's boss around here. I'll really give them a lecture!

April Assertive: I'm glad they came in when I asked them to. I'm really being assertive and honest with them.

"You're late."

You are scheduled to meet a friend for an important meeting. She is an hour late when she arrives. You tell her that you are upset because she is so late, and you would have liked more time to spend with her. She acknowledges your feelings and says she will try to be on time in the future. Do you think to yourself:

Doris Doormat: I'm really pleased that she will make an effort to be on time in the future, but wasn't I awfully aggressive and mean to say anything about it? I hate being so aggressive, so I'll stop demanding things and just hope they work out from now on.

Iris Indirect: She might be on time in the future, but I shouldn't have said anything about it today. It's so embarrassing to have to go out of my way to say something about it. I should just be late next time and see how *she* feels.

Agatha Aggressive: I sure let her off easy. What an inconsiderate woman to be late! I should have really told her off.

April Assertive: I'm really glad that our meeting will be on time in the future, and I'm pleased that I was assertive and mentioned it today. I was really honest and spontaneous, and I really like it.

If Doris' responses sound all too familiar to you, you have been mislabeling assertive behavior as aggressive, bitchy, impolite, nagging, bossy, etc. You are also inhibiting your own assertive behavior by attaching an inappropriate, undesirable label to them. Remember that *aggressive* behavior such as Agatha's could be labeled "nagging," "bossy," or "bitchy"—*not* assertive behavior.

If your labels are more like Iris', you are looking for revenge or trying to elicit guilt rather than rewarding your assertive behavior. You are mislabeling your assertive behavior as too easy or too direct, or as embarrassing. If Agatha's labels resemble yours, you are mislabeling your appropriate assertive behavior as weak, passive or meek. Assertive behavior may seem mild in comparison to your aggressive behavior, but you are inhibiting your assertive responses by mislabeling them. The assertive woman, April, correctly labels her assertive behavior as direct, spontaneous, and honest. She rewards her own assertive behavior. Attach appropriate labels to your assertive behavior, and make a conscious effort to tell yourself you've been assertive. Rewarding your assertive behavior will give you support to attain a very desirable goal—being an assertive woman.

IV. Becoming an Assertive Woman

One's philosophy is not best expressed in words, it is expressed in the choices one makes . . . In the long run, we shape our lives and we shape ourselves. The process never ends until we die. And the choices we make are ultimately our responsibility.
—*Eleanor Roosevelt*

Acquiring new assertive behaviors involves becoming more aware of your own attitudes, actions and reactions, and understanding those that will promote your assertion and those which will delay it. As you find ways to structure your progress, you will also become more aware of the possible consequences of choosing to be assertive.

The assertive woman is not born so; she has learned to behave assertively. In our society, this is no easy accomplishment. Women are viewed stereotypically as passive, submissive, helpless, unadventurous, dependent, emotional, and security-oriented. For a woman to behave assertively and to exhibit positive traits which have been deemed desirable for men only (ambition, autonomy, independence, self-expression) she must risk having her femininity questioned. If a woman behaves in the traditional feminine manner, she then must accept second-class status. As women become increasingly aware of options open to them, remaining traditionally "feminine" can be painful and frustrating. If women choose to explore new alternatives, they may fear the loss of outside support from their families and friends. Given these conditions, it is no wonder that both women and men feel the stress inherent in just coping with their changing environment.

As you begin to behave more assertively, you may find that you are working against old, non-assertive behavior patterns that you learned years before. Applying some basic learning principles will help you to develop and maintain assertive behaviors as you combat old behavior patterns. Using the guidelines in this chapter will prepare the way for your continued success in becoming an assertive woman.

Many social behaviors are learned and practiced over time. You become assertive by paying attention to your attitudes as well as toward specific behaviors. Whether or not the environment will support your newly-adopted behaviors is also an important consideration.

Attitudes

Knowing how you feel about yourself is the first step toward learning assertive behaviors. You should become aware of your attitudes about assertion, seeking to identify which attitudes promote learning a new behavior and which attitudes discourage it.

From childhood women may have developed attitudes that inhibit learning assertiveness. Some of these attitudes are listed below. Which did you grow up with?
- Girls are helpless and need to be protected and taken care of.
- Girls are helpful routinely; boys may choose to help, especially creatively.
- Girls are fearful.
- Boys are independent, courageous and brave; girls are dependent, easily influenced by others.
- Girls should help with home domestic chores; boys should strive more for outside achievement.
- Girls are weak and easily hurt; boys are tough.
- Girls are obedient; boys will be boys.
- Girls who assert themselves are being aggressive.

Your thoughts and attitudes alone can perpetate non-assertive behavior. If you believe it would be *terrible* for you to behave assertively, you aren't likely to give it a try. Exploring the thoughts and attitudes that prevent you from expressing yourself can actually help you to stimulate positive new behaviors. Once you are aware of your attitudes, you have an opportunity to view them more realistically. This concept is central to Albert Ellis' rational therapy approach. For example, Doris Doormat may think to herself:

"If I tried to assert myself in this situation, I know I'd say the wrong thing and people would think I'm stupid and unfeminine. *That would be terrible.* I'd never live through it." By imagining catastrophic consequences, Doris is effectively teaching herself not to be assertive. April would have quite a different attitude: "If I try to assert myself in this situation, I will feel better because I'm saying or doing something. By expressing my views, I know I will benefit."

Try to be aware of the imagined consequences you attach to asserting yourself. If you find you have some attitudes which discourage acting assertively, make a conscious effort to have those *attitudes* work for you instead of against you. Try repeating to yourself, "I will say or do something in this situation because I believe it could be effective. I will benefit from asserting myself." If you practice saying this as you begin new behaviors, it will be easier for you to progress in self-assertion.

Also, try to *visualize* yourself acting assertively and experiencing positive consequences. If you frequently see yourself failing to be assertive, imagine some situations in which you are successfully assertive. As you visualize yourself becoming more positive, your self-image will change also. The more you regard yourself as an assertive woman, the more likely you are to behave assertively.

For many women, attitudes about what is feminine prevent them from behaving assertively. Women who feel it is unfeminine or aggressive to behave assertively have two alternatives: to continue to behave passively and obediently, or to retreat completely from the situation. The result of either approach is to avoid an opportunity to develop assertiveness.

In addition, many women have been trained to be so dependent on others that the prospect of behaving assertively and independently seems to them to be totally out of the question.

Some women are greatly handicapped by considering assertion as an option open to men only. Assertion is not limited to masculine or feminine; we believe it is a human quality, an option available to everyone.

For women, behaving assertively means overcoming old dependencies. You may have avoided acting independently and assertively because of the anxiety or fear involved in changing your behavior. If you consider the anxiety and pain you have felt when you acted non-assertively, you will find that assertion is a welcome alternative.

Behaviors

Learning new behaviors involves three steps:
1. Description or modeling of the behavior;
2. Reinforcing the desirable behavior; and
3. Receiving accurate, rapid feedback.

As you learn assertive behaviors, an awareness of their causes (antecedents) and their results (consequences) is also important.

1. *Description or modeling of the behavior*

Throughout this book we present descriptions and illustrations of appropriate behaviors that will serve as assertive models for you. Before you begin attempting assertion, be sure you understand the difference between assertive and aggressive behaviors. It is also worthwhile to talk with or observe someone whom you feel is an assertive person. Research has shown that learning takes place as a result of observation as well as through descriptions of the appropriate behavior.

2. *Reinforcing the desired behavior*

Your first attempts at assertion should be those which will likely meet with positive consequences. Choose situations in which you are likely to experience control. If you try to tackle more difficult areas too fast, you risk negative consequences which could discourage you from asserting yourself in the future. For example, it would generally be wiser to assertively give a compliment as a beginning, rather than attempt to assertively handle someone who is manipulating you. If you proceed gradually, from initial assertions to increasingly difficult ones, you will increase the probability of becoming an assertive woman. Arrange it initially so you are likely to be rewarded, rather than punished, for your assertive behavior. As you continue to behave assertively, you will find that just the act of being assertive is in itself rewarding. We cannot stress enough that the goal of assertion is not "victory," but being able to express your needs and desires openly and honestly. Remember, the compulsion to "win at all costs" is the burden of the aggressive person.

When you are practicing assertive behaviors, ask a friend to give you feedback on your behavior:

- Did my assertive words match my body image?
- Did I use my voice, gestures, and posture assertively?
- Are there specific areas that need improvement?
- Which ones?

You can also give yourself accurate feedback with the help of a mirror or a tape recorder. Practice assertive behaviors in front of a mirror before you try it in the real situation; use the tape recorder to receive feedback about the tone, volume, and quality of your voice. You may be surprised to discover that your image in the mirror is not as assertive as you had thought.

Combining a knowledge of what assertive behavior is with actually performing it and receiving reinforcement and feedback will provide you with a strong foundation you can build on. It is a good formula to follow as you develop assertive responses. Practice and preparation beforehand will make it much more likely that you will continue to behave assertively. Practice or rehearse your assertive behaviors using the exercises in this book. The more attention you give to practicing assertive behaviors, the more comfortable you will be in asserting yourself.

In spite of your preparation and new knowledge, you may still find it difficult to behave assertively. If you find yourself being generally non-assertive, you may benefit from the extra support and guidance that a professional counselor or therapist can provide. Changing your lifestyle is not easy. Many women have combined other resources to help them become more assertive: the help of professional therapists or facilitators, reading books, attending workshops, or enrolling in classes.

Antecedents and consequences of behavior

Knowing what causes or stimulates your behavior, and being aware of how your behavior affects you and others are both important in learning new behaviors. Specifying the antecedents and the consequences of your behavior can support you in your efforts to be an assertive woman.

Antecedents

People and situations probably cause you to behave in certain patterns. Identifying the ones that have caused you to behave non-assertively in the past will give you direction for behaving assertively in the future. Sharon Bower in her manual, *Learning Assertive Behavior With PALS,* has developed a comprehensive list of people and situations for use in identifying who or what causes women to behave non-assertively. We have condensed it here. Use it as a starting point for developing your awareness of situations you can handle more assertively.

"Who done it?"

Place a check (✓) beside the items that cause you to behave non-assertively. After you have finished, review the items you have checked. You will have a list to use in guiding your progress toward assertive behaviors.

1. *Who* has made you feel passive or non-assertive?
    _____ a spouse?
    _____ children?
    _____ a relative?
    _____ friends?
    _____ an employer? an employee?
    _____ a teacher? a doctor? a police officer?
    _____ a sales clerk? waiters or waitresses?
    _____ an acquaintance?
    _____ other: _____
2. *When* have you felt non-assertive, especially as you *ask* for:
    _____ cooperation from spouse, children, employer, employees?
    _____ a loan of money or an item?
    _____ a favor?
    _____ a job?
    _____ love and attention?
    _____ directions?
    _____ other: _____

3. *What* subject has caused you to behave non-assertively:
_____ sex?
_____ politics?
_____ women's rights?
_____ your accomplishments?
_____ others' accomplishments?
_____ your mistakes?
_____ others' mistakes?
_____ expressing positive feelings?
_____ expressing negative feelings?
_____ other: _____

4. *Size* of the group might be a factor in causing you to behave non-assertively; did the situation involve you and:
_____ one other familiar person?
_____ one other unfamiliar person?
_____ two or more familiar persons?
_____ two or more unfamiliar persons?
_____ a group of familiar persons?
_____ a group of unfamiliar persons?

Consequences

Your behavior has consequences; it does affect other people. Women who have behaved passively for long periods of time usually acknowledge that the behavior of others affects them, but they are seldom aware of the extent to which their passive behaviors affect others. Recognizing the consequences of your behavior is an important element in learning assertive behaviors.

Assertive behavior is likely to have positive consequences. When you assert yourself, you will feel more in control of your life and less helpless and frustrated. While you remain passive, the consequences are likely to be painful for you and for others. Other people may resent you for being so dependent on them or for allowing them to make your decisions for you. They may feel burdened by your non-assertiveness.

There may also be people who have actually encouraged you to behave passively. Your mate, for example, may have reinforced your passive behavior by labeling your assertive attempts as aggressive, or by blaming you for difficulties in your relationship. In such a situation it is understandable that you would feel anxious about asserting yourself, because you have experienced such negative consequences in the past. Consequently, professional counseling or assertive training for the other family members might be recommended. If your family is prepared and willing to try to make some changes themselves, you are likely to benefit, physically and emotionally, from asserting yourself.

To make consequences of your behavior work for you, remember to choose intitial assertions that are likely to result in positive consequences. You will be less likely to be discouraged in the future. Don't attempt more difficult assertions until you have had sufficient practice and preparation, and *feel* comfortable with previous ones.

In summary, your attitudes and previous ways of behaving affect your new attempts to behave assertively. Structuring your learning of assertive behaviors will help you to experience success with few setbacks.

_____ Consider your thoughts and attitudes about being assertive. Which ones encourage and support an assertive image of yourself?

_____ Are you avoiding assertion because you fear disastrous consequences?

_____ Be aware of the situations and people that have caused you to be passive in the past, and use them as reminders to be assertive in the future.

_____ Practice new behaviors that result in positive consequences.

_____ Stay *away* from people who punish your attempts to be assertive. Seek out people who reward your assertive attempts with positive feedback.

_____ Look at becoming assertive as a positive experience, instead of a negative problem-solving venture. Remember, learning to be assertive can be fun!

V. From Apology to Power

> *There is only one way to learn, and that way*
> *is to get down to business. To only talk*
> *about power is useless. If you want to know*
> *what power is, . . . you must tackle*
> *everything yourself.*
> Carlos Casteneda
> Journey to Ixtlan

Apology and powerlessness have characterized the lives of many women for generations. A woman's traditional social role has been a dependent, submissive one. Women have been expected to react rather than act, to have decisions made for them rather than make decisions for themselves. What women seek now is the power to determine the course of their own lives without apology, to make their own decisions, and to be free from the absolute authority of others.

Ever since Eve's temptation of Adam resulted in banishment from the Garden of Eden, women have learned to be accessible to blame.

Stereotypes start early. We hear jokes about mothers-in-law being to blame for family conflict; Jewish mothers being responsible for fostering helplessness and dependency in the their children; women elementary school teachers making "sissies" of little boys. Women have been so involved in defending themselves against these accusations that they have rarely questioned their legitimacy. Instead, they have learned to react with feelings of guilt and apology, and they have incorporated these feelings into many other interpersonal situations.

For example, it is not uncommon to observe a situation in which someone accidently steps on a woman's foot, to which she hastily replies, "Oh! Excuse me! I'm so sorry my feet were in your way. How clumsy of me." Sound familiar?

Developing your sense of power

This chapter is concerned with helping you to develop a sense of personal power. The idea of personal power is so important to effective assertive behavior that it deserves our special emphasis and your alert attention.

We agree with the United Nations' Universal Declaration of Human Rights that all persons have the right to expressing and exercising their personal rights to life and freedom without apology; and that all persons have the right everywhere to be recognized as a person. We further believe that what women have been told about themselves and their powerlessness has been untrue. The question of power is beginning to assume new importance. There seem to be two major aspects of personal power for women: methods of getting it and keeping it, and attitudes about having it and using it.

Personal power is something we all want. Yet women have been denied the opportunity to exercise power; they have been told it isn't "natural" or "feminine" for them to want it. They have swallowed their anxiety, buried their anger, and experienced the personal anguish and disappointment produced by powerlessness and non-assertion. In an article on power, Michael Korda emphasizes that traditionally the exercise of power has been a masculine perogative, but women need a sense of personal power, too. We do not insist that women must compete with men for success, money, prestige, or authority, which are all frequently seen as external barometers of power. Instead, we are concerned with power as a positive, creative force that helps you choose for yourself, gives you a feeling of worth and purpose, and fosters a strong conviction to overcome feelings of anxiety and helplessness.

Women are intimately familiar with the advice "To get, you've got to give." In acquiring a sense of personal power, this advice may be modified: "To get, you've got to give *up* self-denying behavior."

You must learn not to undermine and defeat your attempts to exercise your power.

The need for approval

The need for approval prevents many women from developing a sense of power. Working for others' approval can limit your own autonomy because you voluntarily concede your power to someone else. Doris Doormat, for example, is a reliable, responsible employee. She makes decisions, but once she's made them, she presents them to someone else because she wants that person to tell her she's done a good job, to give her approval. By allowing another person to pass final judgment, Doris effectively limits her own potential autonomy. April Assertive can make decisions without the need to present them to someone else. She uses her own power and resists seeking the familiar comfort of approval. Her autonomy and personal power are more important to her. As an assertive woman, April stands up for what she believes, and makes decisions independently for herself.

Action vs. reaction

Women have traditionally been expected to *react* to situations rather than *act* to change them. Such a self-denying proposition will defeat your attempts to exercise control over your own life. This is a most corrupting kind of powerlessness. Being able to initiate action promotes an assertive attitude and a sense of personal power. An assertive attitude includes autonomy—learning how to set your own limits, making independent decisions, and being free of unnecessary guilt. You acknowledge by your actions that you can run your own life. Here are some familiar situations:

"I'm sorry, but . . ."

The phrase "I'm sorry, but . . ." is a common refrain. Women frequently feel compelled to apologize for saying "no," for exercising their authority, for expressing their anger or for requesting something. A woman's inappropriate use of apology reflects her feelings of powerlessness, indecisiveness, and ambivalence about whether or not she even has the *right* to ask for something, or to disagree. When women apologize unnecessarily, they are really saying, "I know I don't have the *right* to say this, and I don't want to bother you with it, and I'm sorry for saying it, but . . ."

There are legitimate and appropriate occasions for an apology. The legitimate apology conveys an understanding and appreciation of the other person's feelings, such as "I'm very sorry I was late; I must have kept you waiting for an hour." The examples below illustrate inappropriate and appropriate uses of apology.

"Guess who's coming to dinner?"

Situation: Doris Doormat has invited several women to her home for dinner this evening at 7 p.m. They finally arrive at 9, two hours late. The dinner Doris prepared is cold and ruined. One of her guests, Agatha, is critical.

Agatha: "Weren't we invited for dinner, Doris? You didn't plan very well, did you?"

Doris: "Oh, I'm so sorry, Agatha! I feel just awful about this. I'm really sorry to cause such an inconvenience."

In this situation, Doris apologizes inappropriately. It is Agatha and the other guests, who by arriving late, caused Doris the inconvenience. The apology should have come from them.

"Dinner is served—late"

Situation: April Assertive has invited two of her friends to dinner at 7 p.m. She is late coming home, and doesn't arrive until 6:45. When her friends arrive at 7, April is just preparing dinner, which won't be ready until 9.

April: "I'm really sorry that dinner will be late. You must be absolutely starving. How about some cheese and crackers, while we're waiting?"

In this case, April apologizes legitimately to her friends for the late dinner. She acknowledges that they must be hungry and makes a positive suggestion, but she does not over-apologize.

The next time you find yourself apologizing, ask yourself what you are apologizing for:

- Was the apology legitimate and appropriate?

- Did you feel compelled to apologize?

- Did you apologize for something even though you had nothing to be sorry about?

For the assertive woman, every day does not have to be a perpetuation of the oppression of apology.

To move from reaction to action, from apology to power, the assertive woman develops an understanding of power and her relation to it.

The assertive woman knows that the best way to protect her rights is to use them. Becoming comfortable with power and enjoying a feeling of competency will take some practice. You may find yourself struggling against years of apology as a lifestyle. By using the exercises in this chapter you can develop an assertive attitude and experience a feeling of being in control. Before attempting each exercise, remember that it is very important to practice relaxation and simultaneously to imagine yourself successfully completing the exercise. After you are able to fantasize yourself trying the exercise without feeling anxious, try it out alone in front of a mirror. Then you are ready to try it with a friend with whom you feel comfortable, and/or in a relatively safe situation. Do not push yourself too fast and do not try to do the exercise with an intimidating person or in an uncomfortable situation, until you have mastered relaxation and the successful fantasy.

We have emphasized the importance of initiating action. A good way to begin is by initiating and maintaining conversations. You won't have to wait for someone to begin a conversation with you.

"Hi! My name is . . ."

Four suggestions that you can use to initiate a conversation were shown to us by Sherwin Cotler and Julio Guerra, and we recommend them to you. Once the conversation gets going, however, you need to vary these approaches to maintain interest for yourself and the other person. Do not get attached to one favorite approach; use them all, and observe how it feels to be in control.

1. *Ask open-ended questions:* These are questions that require more than a mere "yes" or "no" answer, i.e., questions that begin with *what, when, where, who, why* and *how.* "What kinds of things did you do today?" will elicit much more of a response than "Did you go to work today?"

2. *Listen for free information and comment on it:* Free information is extra information a person tells you that may not have anything to do with the question you asked.

3. *Self-disclosure:* Give free information about yourself. Tell how you feel, what you've been doing, what you believe. This does not mean giving out free information about others or gossiping. Gossiping acts against self-disclosure by preventing you from revealing something about yourself.

4. *Give a compliment:* Saying something that you sincerely appreciate about the other person, or possibly about someone else you both know. This is discussed further in Chapter VI, "Compliments, Criticism, & Rejection." Look for four basic conversational skills in the following dialogue.

"Let's play tennis"

You approach someone you don't know at a party and say:

April: Hi, my name is April. What's yours?

Bill: Bill. Nice to meet you, April.

April: Thank you. Tony told me you're here on your vacation.

Bill: Yes, it's so nice to be off work for two weeks! I'm planning to relax and play a lot of tennis.

April: Tony told me that you're an excellent tennis player. There are several good tennis courts here, and you can play all day and at night too. I just played last night.

Bill: How was it?

April: I had a good time, but I was having some trouble with my serve.

Bill: I know just what you mean. I used to have trouble too, until I learned an easy serve from a great instructor. I'd be happy to teach it to you some time.

April: That would be great. What are you doing tomorrow night?

Getting your questions answered

Have you experienced the problem of asking a question and then allowing yourself to be sidetracked by the other person changing the subject and not answering your question? If so, you are left feeling frustrated, confused, and possibly angry.

Try the following outline suggested by Gerald Piaget, to help you to exercise some control and get your questions answered:

1. Start with a brief, specific question.

2. Picture yourself practicing asking this question of a comfortable person and as you do so practice your relaxation.

3. Put step (2) into action, and ask a friend your question. Instruct your friend to try to avoid answering your question by every means possible until she feels she has run out of excuses and evasive comments. Each time she gives another rationalization, continue to ask the question as if it were the first time it was asked, without varying your voice tone.

4. If you don't receive an appropriate answer, precede your question with "I will repeat the question," or a similar neutral statement, followed by a repetition of the question.

5. If your friend responds with a *feeling* instead of an answer to your question, *acknowledge* the feeling, but continue to repeat your question.

6. When a direct answer is given, acknowledge the answer in a neutral, non-judgmental way, "Thank you for telling me."

7. If in evading answering your question your friend makes insulting or other negative remarks, you may follow your acknowledgement by telling your friend how you feel about these remarks. You can do this assertively, without punishing your friend for not answering you honestly. If you do punish your friend, you will inhibit her/his chances of being open with you in the future. What you are concerned with is your right to exercise your power to have your questions answered. So, remember the assertive woman remains non-judgmental and non-abusive, and keeps her voice evenly modulated—not loud or angry.

This example of how to get your question answered came up in one of our groups:

"Are you having an affair?"

In our workshops, this situation has come to our attention frequently. The woman has usually experienced a great deal of emotional pain, and has attempted to deal with it by ignoring it, by playing a martyr role, or by fighting fire with fire. At this point, she is ready to try the alternative of being assertive. The following dialogue illustrates a classic assertive response to an emotionally-charged situation. Each woman must tailor her response to her own needs and style, rather than conforming to a general model. This may mean that her assertiveness is interrupted by angry outbursts or crying. Remember that to be assertive does not mean to be perfect.

April: I have been concerned lately about the amount of time you are away from home. You have been telling me that you are busy, have to work late, etc., but I have the feeling you are holding back on me. Are you having an affair?

Lover: Don't be ridiculous. I've got important work to do. It takes too much time to explain it to you. You don't understand.

April: I feel like you're being evasive with me, and I am very concerned about what's happening. I will repeat my question. Are you having an affair?

Lover: How many times have I told you not to bug me with your stupid questions? I'm really angry! Why don't you trust me?

April: I know that you are angry about my asking you the same question over again. I really do want to trust you. I can trust you when you are open with me. I would feel more comfortable knowing the truth and being given the choice to deal with it, rather than being in the dark and feeling anxious and insecure. I would like to know if you are having an affair.

Lover: You really know how to back somebody up against the wall, don't you? You must really get a kick out of playing Sherlock Holmes. I've had enough of your nagging. How do you think it makes me feel to be interrogated like this and subjected to your high pressure tactics? I suppose your friends put you up to this.

April: I want you to feel comfortable about discussing this with me. The last thing I want to do is threaten you. It is really important to me to clear up this distance between us. I would like to know where I stand, so it is very important for me to know if you're having an affair. Are you?

Lover: Well, just remember that you asked for it! Yes, I am having an affair. I hope you're happy now that you squeezed it out of me.

April: I appreciate your telling me, even though it doesn't make me happy to know that you're having an affair. I feel at least now we can begin an honest discussion of our feelings.

Remember that the content in this exercise is extremely meaningful. It is important to choose your words in such a way that you are not accusatory, for example by saying, "I feel" instead of "you make me feel." Even though the other person may insult you, it is important to be concerned with your feelings rather than letting yourself get sidetracked by name-calling or other manipulative devices.

You have a right to ask questions and to expect direct answers, and you should give such answers yourself. However, there are times when you will not want to be forced to answer questions. Self-assertion will give you the power to decide.

Choosing not to answer questions

Now that you have practiced getting your questions answered, consider what you do whenever you are in the opposite position. How do you respond when someone is asking you a question you do *not* want to answer? Perhaps the question is irrelevant, embarrassing, intimidating, or very uninteresting. How do you handle this situation? Try a method that has worked for us.

First of all, be sure you understand the question. If you do not, then clarify it by repeating it back to your questioner. Once it is clarified and you are aware that you still do not feel comfortable in answering the question, make a simple, direct statement saying that you do not want to answer it. If the questioner persists, you may express how this question or the persistence of the questioner makes you feel. Then repeat again that you do not want to answer the question.

"Where have you been . . .?"

Situation: A single career woman just took a few days off from work to have an abortion. There are a couple of people with whom she works that she doesn't want to know about her abortion. However, she had some obvious signs of pregnancy before she had the abortion, and these people were acting quite nosey and suspicious.

Nosey: Oh, April, you look a little pale. You must have been pretty sick to have stayed out for three days. Would you like to talk about it?

April: I'm not sure what you mean by "it." Could you be a little more specific?

Nosey: Well, some of us noticed that you were nauseated a few mornings here at work. And your clothes didn't seem to be fitting quite the same, if you know what I mean. Well, what I'm trying to say is—April, did you have an abortion?

April: I really feel uncomfortable with your asking me what I feel is a very personal question, and I don't want to answer it.

Nosey: Of course, I know it is rather personal, but we're asking only because we care about you. Is there anything we can do?

April: It really makes me angry for you to persist in prying into my personal life. I do not feel it is necessary to answer your question.

Nosey: I don't see why not. Everybody knows anyway.

April: I do not want to discuss your question any further. I am going to resume working, which I feel is the appropriate thing for us to do.

Write down three questions that you anticipate people may ask you that you do not want to answer. Then role-play the situation and practice *not* answering the question by using the process described in the previous exercise.

Eliminating "I'm sorry, but . . ."

For a week, keep a daily count of how many times you say "I'm sorry, but . . ." If your highest daily count is 18, for example, then begin your second week by trying to reduce the times you say it to an achievable goal, say by two each day. By persistent awareness you will be able to eventually go for a week without saying it at all. Try to reduce your inappropriate use of apology in these three basic situations that can repeat themselves over and over again:

1) when making a request,
2) when stating what you are going to do, and
3) when stating what you are not going to do.

"Doctor knows best"

Situation: A woman has discovered she has lumps in her breasts. She is in the office of her gynecologist (who happens to be a man). She needs to request information.

Doris: *I'm* really *sorry*, Doctor, *but* tell me what I should do. You know best.

April: Doctor, I would like you to explain to me in detail all the pros and cons of my situation, so I can make the best decision for me.

Now, ask yourself—why should anyone be sorry for asking a very important health care question of her doctor? The assertive woman uses her right to be in control of her body and to know what's happening to her, especially in situations where she may have to decide about a mastectomy or other serious surgery.

From our experience with hundreds of women it is clear that the woman who can handle this type of situation assertively with powerful authority figures (doctors, ministers, law enforcement officers) can readily apply the same behaviors to everyday situations with family members, close friends and others with whom she is more comfortable.

"Simon, may I take two giant steps?"

Situation: A woman has recently become familiar with the idea of consciousness-raising groups and has heard that one will be forming in her neighborhood. She is very excited about joining and wants to tell her mate what she is going to do.

Doris: Honey, there's a C-R group forming right in our block, and well, they meet one night a week . . . only for two hours though. What I'm trying to say is well, *I'm sorry, but* I'd like to go to the group, maybe just once, if you don't mind.

April: Honey, I want to discuss with you your feelings about my joining a C-R group here in the neighborhood. They'll meet one night a week and I feel it would be a very meaningful experience for me. I'd really like to go.

Here again there is no need for the assertive woman to apologize for wanting to do something that will add to her personal growth. Of course, she remains open to discuss her mate's possible objections, but emphasizes the importance to her of joining the group. She is willing to discuss her mate's possible feelings of being left out or threatened, but she continues to negotiate for herself.

"Sure, no problem"

Situation: This topic comes up quite frequently in our women's classes, especially with secretaries.

The boss (usually male) has just asked his secretary if she wouldn't mind during her lunch break exchanging some merchandise his wife bought. He then adds that he'd like her to try to get back from lunch *early* because he has some extra typing for her that must be done right away. She wants to tell him that she is not going to do it.

Doris: Oh, *I'm sorry, but* I was going to have lunch with a friend I haven't seen in years who's in town for the day. But, I guess I could call her and cancel our plans. Yes, I guess I'll do that. Sure, it's no problem. Where do you want me to go?

April: I had made plans with a good friend that I haven't seen in years. She will only be in town today, and it is very important to me that I see her. I know that you are rushed and don't have time to return the merchandise yourself. However, if it is necessary to return it today, perhaps I can do it later, as well as the extra typing. Also, I would like to discuss with you being compensated adequately for extra jobs that I do overtime. I value my lunch hour and being able to leave the office on time too.

"Do you have the nerve?"

Here is another action exercise we have developed to help you to gain confidence in taking the initiative—by acting instead of waiting to react. Choose at least three out of the five following situations and rank them according to how uncomfortable the thought of doing them makes you feel, *A* being the *least* uncomfortable and *F* being the *most* uncomfortable. Then, starting with A, decide how you are going to go about doing something active about it instead of waiting to see what the other person does. You can write a script before you try it or role-play what you are going to say first. Try to visualize what the assertive woman would do:

_____ Make an appointment with your employer, teacher, or family to let them know that you feel you are doing a fine job, instead of waiting to react only after somebody notices.

_____ Your children or someone else's children are hassling you. You tell them that you want their attention and take responsibility for telling them how you are feeling and that you want them to stop hassling you right now. Do *not* threaten them with "Wait until your father/mother hears about this," do not wait until somebody else takes the responsibility, do not react with pent-up frustration and complaining.

_____ Phone a woman or a man whom you have never phoned about something you want to tell her/him instead of waiting for her/him to call you.

_____ Somebody is going to make a request of you, perhaps to buy or borrow something or to ask a favor of you. If you do not feel like buying it or doing it, say so right away instead of letting your anxiety build as you wait for the person to ask you.

_____ You need to talk to your lover/mate about an important feeling you have, perhaps about sex. Set up the right time and place and initiate the conversation. Do not passively wait for the right time and place to just happen, or for the other person to talk about it first.

_____ Returning an item to the store, even though you don't have the sales slip, or you have procrastinated for weeks or months about returning it.

In this chapter we have tried to specify some ways in which the assertive woman can get in touch with her own sense of personal power, as well as point out ways for her to implement that power. As you complete the exercises you will also begin to feel more in control of your own life and will be aware of how apology may have left you inhibited and powerless in the past.

Keep in mind that power doesn't guarantee that you will always get what you want. You are on your way to becoming an assertive woman as you begin to realize that power begins with a feeling of confidence. This confidence develops from the conviction that to be assertive is in itself more valuable than winning. Your assertiveness alone will help you to earn the reputation of a winner.

VI. Compliments, Criticism and Rejection

*"I could live for two months on a good
compliment."—Mark Twain*

*"The more active and fruitful your life, the
more you will receive criticism."
—Anonymous*

Compliments

Before you can comfortably give and receive compliments
assertively, it is important to know how you feel about compliments
in general. The assertive woman regards a compliment as a sincere,
specific expression of appreciation. Compliments, not always sincere, abound in the "Compassion Trap"—when we are compulsively
taking care of others and making them feel good, frequently at our
own expense. Because the Compassion Trap is so much a part of most
women's lives, it is common to see women using compliments to
cheer someone up or to compensate for negative feelings about a
person. While her intentions are good, a woman runs the risk of
being superficial and being "found out." This has happened many
times and accounts for the accusations that women are "false
flatterers." Furthermore, women are expected to be easy prey to
flattery because they are supposedly "so vain" and in need of
constant reassurance. Fortunately, neither women nor men are born
to be flattered. Since we learn false flattery and acting in accordance
with the expectations of others, we can also learn to give and to
receive sincere compliments.

For example, instead of telling the depressed woman in the office, whom you like, that she looks nice today and has on a lovely outfit (she is obviously depressed and looking dowdy), you should be honest with her. You could say that you have noticed the woman is feeling down, and that you are concerned about her because you like her and consider her a special person.

Another obstacle to giving and receiving compliments is that many of us have been programmed to believe that it is immodest and unladylike to acknowledge a compliment, and that the proper response when complimented is to protest and show embarrassment. This response usually has an unfortunate effect on the complimenter, who feels put down or uneasy for having said "the wrong thing." It is unlikely that this person will want to risk saying anything nice to you again.

Sometimes in our society we rely too heavily on gifts and material things (including commercial "mushy" cards) to show our appreciation for another person, because we do not feel comfortable in saying or writing our own original words of appreciation in an assertive way. There are even times when a compliment can be non-verbal: a warm touch or pat on the back, a smile, a nod, a warm handshake, giving an O.K. sign and a wink, etc.

If you feel uncomfortable upon receiving a compliment is it because you feel obligated to return the compliment to the other person? It is not necessary to reciprocate with a compliment, but it is important to acknowledge what the person has said to you. This can be done either verbally or nonverbally with a smile or nod of recognition. If you choose to acknowledge the compliment verbally, it is enough to say thank-you. You may also add some free information regarding how you feel about what was said. This technique is mentioned as an alternative way to initiate a conversation in Chapter V, "From Apology to Power." Giving free information after you acknowledge a compliment is a nice way of letting a person know that her/his compliment was meaningful to you. This is how it works:

"April, I really like the way you said 'no' to that salesman. You didn't beat around the bush at all, or let him get a word in edgewise."

"Thanks, Linda. It has taken me a while to learn how to say 'no' assertively, and I'm really beginning to have confidence in myself now. It really makes me feel good that you noticed."

Developing confidence in compliments

Use this checklist to develop your ability to give and receive compliments. Work at it, and as you master each item, check it off the list.

_____ Try to avoid falling into the Compassion Trap and giving inappropriate compliments or false flattery in an attempt to make someone feel good.

_____ Give sincere compliments as expressions of your appreciation.

_____ Be specific about what you are complimenting.

_____ Acknowledge a compliment given to you either verbally or non-verbally.

_____ Do not get embarrassed or put down by the person complimenting you.

_____ Do not feel obligated to give a compliment in return for one.

Criticism

The inhibition we experience with giving and receiving compliments we also experience with giving criticism. Probably the prime fear that keeps many women from giving or accepting criticism is the fear of rejection. When your self-esteem is low, it does not take too much to paralyze you with anxiety and fear at the moment of making or receiving critical remarks. So, as your confidence level gets higher while you are becoming assertive, your ability to evaluate criticism objectively will become clearer and stronger. When you are as non-assertive as Doris, you tend to evaluate what people say to you, or what you say, in terms of your own feelings of worthlessness. However, when you are assertive like April, your basic self-image remains strong and intact, while you are able to look at your own faults and share openly with others those things about them that you do not like. You can do this without being rejected by others. In fact, being assertive in giving and receiving criticism will earn you respect, and people will turn toward you rather than away from you.

Another element that makes criticism so hard to take is the element of surprise. Usually the criticism that is the least expected is the one that takes us completely off guard and hurts the most. To overcome the fear of criticism, then, it is important to set up a step-by-step process that will gradually desensitize you to critical remarks, whether anticipated or unexpected.

First of all, this process involves taking a close look at yourself. Secondly, it involves preparing in advance for three possible types of criticism that you might receive: the unrealistic criticism, the put-down, and the valid criticism. However, the assertive woman is careful not to over-prepare or to feel that she must be constantly on guard.

The unrealistic criticism is one that is utterly ridiculous to the point of being the opposite of the truth, e.g. Agatha calling a slim person a "big, fat slob." The put-down may have an element of truth, but it is said in such a way that is it patronizing and/or insulting rather than a legitimate criticism, e.g., Iris saying to someone who is overweight, "Why don't you have a banana split? A few extra pounds here or there doesn't matter when you're fat!" Lastly, the valid criticism is one which is realistic and is stated in a straightforward, assertive manner, e.g. April saying to an overweight person, "I have noticed that you have gained some extra weight. You really looked better and healthier before."

Check your C.Q. (criticism quotient)

Use our checklist to determine how sensitive you are to the different types of criticism. Put a "plus" (+) by those that you handle assertively, a "minus" (-) by those that you avoid handling at all, and a check (✔) by those that you face but handle awkwardly.

_____ Someone criticizes you about a fault that you cannot deny is yours.

_____ You give somebody an honest criticism of what you see as a legitimate problem.

_____ Someone criticizes you for an act that you know without a doubt doesn't apply to you and is ridiculous.

_____ Someone has put you down in an indirect way; there may be some truth to the put-down, but it's basically unfair.

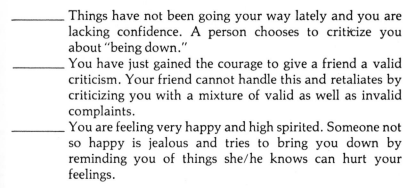

_____ Things have not been going your way lately and you are lacking confidence. A person chooses to criticize you about "being down."

_____ You have just gained the courage to give a friend a valid criticism. Your friend cannot handle this and retaliates by criticizing you with a mixture of valid as well as invalid complaints.

_____ You are feeling very happy and high spirited. Someone not so happy is jealous and tries to bring you down by reminding you of things she/he knows can hurt your feelings.

Be aware of how you have marked the above examples because this will be important in how you complete the exercise on criticism at the end of the chapter.

Rejection

The assertive woman wants to avoid being rejected as a person, but she is aware that it is often natural and unavoidable to have her ideas or acts rejected. The most common form of rejection occurs when someone says "no" in response to your idea, request, or action. Children often find it exasperating to accept "no's" and frequently women do, too. Why is this? With some women, as with children, the need to seek approval appears to be quite strong. Whenever a woman is dependent, it follows that she needs the approval of the person she's dependent upon. Like Doris, she assumes that the other person knows best and elevates this person to a position of authority over her. Thus, like a child, she is vulnerable to fits of resentment and/or rebellion whenever she is told "no." The assertive woman accepts a "no" as meaning "no" to the specific situation, instead of feeling that she is being rejected as a person. Nevertheless, it is possible that the other person may wish to convey that you are "worthless." But, if you are feeling good about yourself, you will not accept this interpretation of you. The assertive woman is able to accept some "no's", because she finds her reward primarily in asserting herself and not just in getting what she wants.

A rejection checklist

Use the following checklist to determine in what ways you may fear rejection. Put a check (✔) in front of each item that causes you to feel rejected regardless of its truth. Put a plus (+) before each item that you can handle assertively.

_____ Your parents or spouse tell you that you are stupid and can't do anything right.

_____ Your lover criticizes your appearance.

_____ A friend says she or he is busy and cannot go with you someplace you wanted to go.

_____ Your child or another's child tells you that you're mean and that she/he hates you.

_____ Someone whose intelligence you respect tells you that your latest brainstorm isn't a good idea.

_____ You're playing a game where sides are chosen by leaders— you're last to be picked.

_____ In a group you make an important statement which is ignored.

_____ You have completed a job as well as you can, but you are told to do it over because it could be better.

_____ You look for physical affection from someone you love who is too busy to give it to you at the moment.

_____ You have asked someone to do a special favor for you, and they refuse.

_____ A significant person in your life forgets your birthday or anniversary.

_____ You apply for a job or admission to a certain school or organization, and you are turned down.

Review the items that cause you to feel anxious and fearful about rejection. If you feel discouraged about the way you answered, the first exercise below will be a good antidote.

Action exercises

Like yourself first

Fill in the blanks with ten positive statements about yourself—things you like about *you* as a person, e.g. "I like the fact that I'm trying to become a more assertive person." Stand in front of a mirror and read each item on your list aloud. While practicing good eye contact and smiling appropriately, acknowledge each compliment that you give yourself either verbally or non-verbally. Practice adding some free information to some of your "thank-you's."

1. _____

2. _____

3. _____

4. _____

5. _____

6. _____

7. _____

8. _____

9. _____

10. _____

This is not only a good list to refer to when you feel rejected. Use it to gain confidence in self-assertion. Refer to the list daily and add to it regularly by telling someone, in regular conversation, something positive about yourself.

Giving and receiving compliments

Try giving and receiving spontaneous compliments with a friend or in your women's group. If you try this in a group, have each woman turn to the woman on her right to give her a compliment. After the woman acknowledges the compliment, continue around the circle until you are all feeling quite comfortable with both giving and receiving. Be sure to give each other feedback: first, on positives about the way in which compliments are delivered or received; then, give each other specific suggestions for improvement that might be necessary.

Giving and receiving criticism

In her paper, "Techniques of Assertive Training in Groups," Pamela E. Butler of The Behavior Institute, Sausalito, California, suggests an exercise for dealing with either unrealistic or realistic criticism. This can be done with a friend or in a group; the following example is adapted from Butler's work.

Take at least 15 minutes and write two separate lists with spaces for 5 to 10 items on each list. Title the first list "Unrealistic Criticisms" and write down what you feel would be ridiculous criticisms of yourself. On the second list, "Realistic Criticisms," write down things that you feel are quite valid criticisms of yourself. Then exchange both lists with another person and take turns reading to one another from your lists, alternating preposterous and realistic items while being as believable and dramatic as possible.

Whenever you are confronted with an unrealistic criticism, contradict it openly, as in the following example:

"Why don't you try social work?"

School counselor: "April, I think your decision to become a psychiatrist is impractical. You aren't good at science and math. Why don't you try social work?

April: "That is the most unfair thing I've heard all day! My abilities in math and science are very strong, and I think becoming a psychiatrist is a practical goal for me."

On the other hand, when responding to a realistic criticism, the assertive woman will acknowledge the criticism as being valid and then may add a statement about how she is working on that problem and is trying to change. Or, she may say that she is aware that a trait bothers others, but that it doesn't bother her and she's really not motivated to do anything about it now. For example, April's reply to her school counselor may sound like this:

April: "You're right about science and math not being my strongest subjects. However, I've arranged for individual tutoring and plan to master those subjects. I will do whatever I can to make sure I can reach my goal to be a psychiatrist."

Besides the unrealistic criticism and the realistic criticism, there is a third type of criticism that we refer to as the "put-down." Although there is an element of truth in the put-down, it is an insult nonetheless; how one responds to it may not seem as clear-cut. There are several levels to this skill. Doris, of course, responds in a completely passive way by either agreeing with the put-down or not being able to say a thing and being totally immobilized. Iris may smile while doing something in a nonverbal, under-handed way to get revenge. Agatha naturally would use counter-aggression ("fighting fire with fire") to get even. The highest level of skill however, is using humor. This is April's response. The use of humor can put an end to the other person's aggression toward you, as well as demonstrate your assertiveness.

Consider, for example, this version of the previous dialogue between April and her school counselor:

School counselor: "April, I think your decision to become a psychiatrist is impractical. Girls just can't weather the strain of *tough* math and science classes. Besides, you'd probably drop out to get married."

April: "It's true that math and science are not my best subjects, which is why I'm not wanting to pursue a career as a mathematician or scientist. However, I feel I've got what it takes to become a good psychiatrist. There are many women psychiatrists who are demonstrating that women can handle the strain of being doctors, not to mention the strain of working with some *male chauvanist* patients."

Putting down putdowns

The "Feminist Invention Group" has put out a little booklet titled "Here are the Answers to those Male Chauvinist Putdowns." Here are a couple of examples from the book:

Putdown	Retort
"Nothing's worse than an old woman trying to look young."	"It's worse for men . . . they age from the bottom up."
"There's the Women's Libber."	"Say it again, I love it!" or "Relax. We'll liberate *you* next."

We have collected the following putdowns from our workshops:

Putdown	Retort
"Are you a Women's Libber?"	"Is *libber* something you serve with bacon or onions?"
"So what if you're a doormat. Just stop it!"	"It's not easy when you have a Ph.D. in ring kissing."
"With those pants on, you look like a dike."	"Well, at least I don't need a zipper up front in case I spring a leak!"
"What're you doin' tonight, baby?"	"Make me an offer I can't refuse!"
"When you swear, you don't sound like a lady."	"L-A-D-Y is a four letter word."
"We can't hire a woman, she'll get sick every month with her period."	"According to U.S. Dept. of Labor, men have a higher sickness rate than women. I guess *their* periods are worse."
"You did a great job *for a woman.*"	"*For a man* you don't seem to be too handicapped yourself."
"She looks so old she must live at 'Menopause Manor'."	"That's a more respectable 'house' than the potbellied playboy's club."

If humor is something that you feel you have to work on, you can always say assertively, "I feel put down by your remark." Giving an "I message" can be just as potent as humor and may nip the putdown in the bud. However, humor does wonders for easing tensions on both sides. We will take a closer look at this in Chapter XI, "Humor—I'm Funny, You're Sarcastic."

Use the following blanks to fill in your own list of putdowns that you have encountered, and see if you can come up with some humorous retorts. This exercise can be a lot of fun to work on in a group.

Putdown   **Retort**

1. _____   _____
   _____   _____
   _____   _____
2. _____   _____
   _____   _____
   _____   _____
3. _____   _____
   _____   _____
   _____   _____
4. _____   _____
   _____   _____
   _____   _____

We would enjoy receiving a copy of your list and adding to our collection of putdowns and responses.

Getting rid of your censor

Here is a group exercise that we learned from Gerald Piaget which will help you to desensitize yourself from giving compliments and criticisms, and aid you in being more spontaneous and open. It involves getting rid of the censor inside your head. Your censor tells you to be overly cautious and not risk saying the wrong thing.

Have one person stand before each person in the group one-by-one and quickly blurt out a few adjectives and nouns—positive and negative—that describe what she notices about each person. Stay away from phrases and sentences and just use one-worders. Move quickly from person to person and have each person take a turn. For example, you may look at a person and say, "short, warm smile, fuzzy, serious, unpredictable, bald, plump, caring, social, bright colors, fifty-ish," etc. The person being spoken to remains neutral and does not comment on anything said about her. Have each person try this until she feels she can be spontaneous with her remarks.

Then think about how comfortable or uncomfortable this exercise was for you. It's even better if you can talk about it with someone. Be specific about what types of words cause you the most trouble—negative or positive or both. Try this exercise again until you feel that you have reached a level of spontaneity that is right for you.

Accepting "no" for an answer

Make a list with three columns: who, what and when, as Sharon Bower and others suggest. Under "who" write down the names of people who you are sensitive about rejecting you. Under "what" list specific situations in which you feel most vulnerable to a "no" response. And finally under "when" write down the times in which you feel most threatened by hearing a "no." Then order these, putting the ones that cause you the least anxiety on top of the list as #1, and continue numbering until you end with the most threatening who, what, and when at the bottom.

Sample:

WHO   (children, employer, friend, husband, other(s)_____)

WHAT   (asking for help around the house, asking for time off, expecting company, making love, other(s)_____)

WHEN   (at home at dinnertime, at work during a hectic day, or chores have piled up around the house, when feeling down, others(s)_____)

Now that you have the above samples, fill in the following blanks with your own lists, ordering them from the least anxiety provoking to the most threatening:

	Who	What	When
Least			
Most			

After you have completed and ordered your list, role-play these situations with a friend or in a group starting with #1 in each column. Keep practicing until you feel comfortable with hearing a "no" from your partner. Then move on to #2. Each time you hear a "no" think to yourself, "I am O.K. for making this request. I am not being rejected as a person; only my *request* is being rejected. I can make this request at another time, and it may be accepted. I feel good about asserting myself and expressing my needs clearly."

In summary, the assertive woman can give, as well as receive, a compliment sincerely and specifically. She avoids giving inappropriate compliments often times caused by her being in the Compassion Trap. Not only can she accept a compliment without embarrassment, but she rarely feels obligated to give a compliment in return for one.

Whereas Doris Doormat feels powerless when criticized and accepts most criticism as further proof of her worthlessness, April Assertive is able to choose how she will react to criticism. She decides whether or not a criticism is unrealistic, valid, or an indirect put-down and responds accordingly. April openly contradicts the unrealistic, acknowledges the valid, and uses humor or an "I message" to counteract the put-down. Besides knowing how to react to criticism, the assertive woman feels free and spontaneous in initiating valid criticisms when she feels it's appropriate.

Iris learns to speak openly and directly and spontaneously. Agatha recognizes her habit of using put-downs and learns that they harm her more than they affect her supposed victims. She develops the ability to make her compliments direct and appropriate and to eliminate the sarcasm and put-downs in her criticism, as opposed to rejection of her totally as a human being. She is comfortable in accepting some "no's" and finds her reward in asserting herself primarily instead of feeling good only if she gets what she wants.

As you can see in this chapter, being assertive sometimes involves defending yourself against attack. At other times, assertion requires that you reach out to others in a positive way. Becoming an assertive woman, therefore, means understanding and learning not only defensive behaviors, but positive approach behaviors as well.

VII. Saying "No"

"The Queen turned crimson with fury, and after glaring at her [Alice] for a moment like a wild beast, began screaming, "Off with her head! Off with—"
"Nonsense!" said Alice, and the Queen was silent.
—Lewis Carroll
Alice in Wonderland

Being "feminine" has often meant that a woman is submissive and indecisive, and that when she says "no" she *really* means "yes!" It is hardly surprising, therefore, that women find it very difficult to say "no." Since women continuously encounter requests from others to do something for them or advertisements insisting that women buy something, it is an enormous handicap for a woman not to be able to say "no."

A woman unable to say "no" may become a "Super Mom" and take on the appearance of an octopus, intent on doing eight different things at once. This woman never says "no"; she just gets busier and busier. Advertising campaigns are geared around a woman's inability to say "no." In fact, much of the buying and selling economy of this country depends on purchases of unnecessary products by women.

Yet, there is a good deal of resistance from women to learn how to say "no." One of the biggest reasons for not saying "no" is the "Compassion Trap"—taking care of someone else's needs despite of your own needs. For Doris, it is easier to say "yes" rather than deal with the guilt she may feel after refusing someone. Or, she may resist the fact that she has the right to evaluate a situation herself and the right to disagree with the person who is making the request of her. Doris lacks confidence in her own decision-making power. She feels worthless in comparison to others and feels that their needs are naturally more worthwhile than her own. Doris perpetuates this sexism by believing that, because she is a woman, it is "normal" to have people take advantage of her. Like Doris, some women often say "yes" to avoid any conflict or encounter with another person. Others fear that refusal can lead to violence toward them or toward a loved one.

Our purpose in writing this particular chapter is to encourage every woman to feel free to say "no" and to exercise her right to refusal. We believe that the assertive woman can earn a great deal of respect and overcome feelings of powerlessness by exercising her right to refuse. Most negative repercussions can be avoided if the refusal is done assertively. In other words, what matters is *how* you say "no" rather than the fact that you have said it. Here are some steps to help overcome the problem you may have of feeling guilty when you say "no."

Four ways to say "No"

First of all, one of the most difficult hurdles to overcome is in assessing whether or not the other person's request of you is reasonable or unreasonable. This can be tricky. We as women must stop looking to the other person to find out if the request is reasonable. The mere fact that the request was made means that the person has decided that she/he wants something from you regardless of its reasonableness. Therefore, the assertive woman looks inside herself to find the answer to whether or not this is a reasonable request. If you find yourself hesitating or hedging, this may be a clue that you want to refuse. If you feel cornered, or trapped, or you notice a tightness or nervous reaction in your body, this may also mean that someone is requesting something unreasonable of you. You feel "uptight." Sometimes you may be genuinely confused or unsure because you just do not have enough information to go on in order to know whether something unreasonable is being asked of you.

Second, you need to assert your right to ask for more information and clarification. Women have often been conditioned to make judgments based on whatever is presented to us. Many of us grew up under the influence of such dicta as "Children should be seen and not heard," or under religious demands that we accept what we have heard as the truth, that to doubt or question is sinful, or that to be submissive and unquestioning was "ladylike." Nevertheless, the first step in asserting yourself when a request is made of you is to make sure you have all the facts. April does not commit herself to a yes or no until she fully understands what is being asked of her.

Third, practice saying "no." Once you understand the request and decide you do not want to do it or buy it, say no firmly and calmly. It is crucial that you give a simple "no" rather than a long-winded statement filled with excuses, justifications, and rationalizations about why you are saying "no." It is enough that you do not want to do this, simply because you do not want to do it. You can accompany your refusal with a simple, straight-forward explanation of what you are feeling. A direct explanation is assertive, while many indirect and misleading excuses are non-assertive and can get you into a lot of trouble by leaving you open for debate.

Fourth, learn to say "no" without saying "I'm sorry, but . . . ." Saying "I'm sorry" frequently weakens your stand and the other person, especially Iris, may be tempted to play on your guilt feelings. When the assertive woman evaluates a situation carefully and decides the best thing for her is to say no, then she has nothing to be sorry about. In fact, April feels strong and happy with her decisions to say no.

The broken record technique

Whenever a person like Agatha does not accept your assertive refusal and resorts to high-pressure tactics with you, you can use the "broken record" technique which other clinicians such as Wanderer, Cotler and Guerra, employ to handle this problem. What you do is simply become a "broken record" and repeat your original assertive refusal each time the person tries another manipulation to persuade you to change your mind. If you remain firm with your original statement, and resist the temptation to answer "Why?," or respond to possible insults, the person will soon run out of new materials and give up. If you tire before this happens, you can end the conversation or change it to another topic.

"You won't mind, will you?"

Imagine the following situation: You have a close friend who has three small children. She has frequently called on you to watch them for a couple of hours at a time, since she is in real estate part-time and has to see potential customers at a minute's notice and at odd hours. You are home anyway, so she feels you will not mind watching them. However, she has gotten tied up lately and often her two hours drags on for six or seven. You are stuck without being able to reach her by phone; consequently you do not get to complete what you have to do. She calls you on the day you have set aside to clean out your garage and prepare for a garage sale. What would you do? Let's see how April would handle this situation.

Jan: "Oh, April, I really have a big buyer today. This one could get me out of debt. You wouldn't mind watching my children for a while, would you?"

April: "What do you mean by 'a while'? How long will you be gone?

Jan: "Oh, I don't know exactly. This is a hot one though, and it shouldn't take more than an hour or two."

April: "Let me think a moment . . . Lately, Jan, when I have watched the kids, you have gotten tied up for longer than you expected and I have no way to phone you. So, I really cannot risk being tied up with the kids today, and I will have to say 'no'."

Jan: "April, what can I say? I need your help so that I can make this sale."

April: "I really have to say 'no', Jan.

Jan: "Well, I suppose I could call a sitter."

April: "That would be great! Let me know whether or not you close the deal."

Exercising your right to refusal and giving yourself time to evaluate requests made of you are both active ways to protect your resources. Any valuable esource, when drawn upon frequently, will become depleted within a short time. When that resource is your energy, time, or love, knowing how to protect it is vitally important to your happiness. Personal strengths can become heavy liabilities if care is not taken to protect them.

When you have overextended yourself physically, your body will automatically begin protecting itself by signalling you to stop. You catch a cold, feel run down, or easily become fatigued. When you have rested, you can resume physical activity at a sensible pace. Your body won't always tell you right away when you are pushing the limits of your emotional resources; but if you frequently feel too busy, overworked, irritable, or "hassled", chances are good that you and/or others have drawn too heavily on your strengths and you need to go about restoring yourself. When your old self tempts you to say yes, be assertive with yourself, and say no.

Saying "no" to things you really enjoy is an especially difficult, but sometimes necessary assertion to preserve and to maintain your enjoyment of them. Many women in our workshops tell us that they have paid a high price for taking on too much at one time. Too much of a good thing can result in painful consequences.

"Enough is enough."

Kim, a college student, was an active participant in several major campus organizations. She maintained a high scholastic average and spent several hours each day studying before attending one of her many meetings. Kim's reputation as a "natural leader" grew along with her list of organization meetings and appointments. Kim was vitally interested and involved in all of her activities. She didn't want to drop any of them, even though she frequently felt too tired to enjoy an evening out with her friends. After one particularly exhausting week, Kim decided to see a doctor for a routine check-up. Kim was found to have mononucleosis, and as a result she was instructed to withdraw from college for the semester to have complete rest. For Kim, trying to do too much resulted in not being able to do anything at all.

Beth is a talented photographer who enjoys her work. She encountered such an enthusiastic demand for her services that she spent every minute trying to satisfy all of the requests for her time. She didn't want to refuse anyone because she really loved photography, and enjoyed spending time on it. But Beth's talent also became her liability as her schedule became heavier and heavier, and her free time began to disappear. Beth wisely began to refuse some photography assignments, worked to stabilize her schedule, and successfully protected her talent and her enjoyment.

"Think it over"

Giving yourself time to evaluate requests made of you will also protect your resources. You don't have to commit yourself to something as soon as you are asked to do it. "Let me think it over and get back to you" is an important statement to make. Before you make your decision, ask yourself:

- Do I really want to do this, or am I really trying to please someone else?
- What will I receive for my participation?
- If I decide to do this, will it continue to be rewarding or will it become oppressive?

After you have had time to decide if you can really comply with the request, you can choose what you will do having had the benefit of time for careful consideration. The assertive woman is able to preserve her resources by not over-committing herself.

Saying "No" without guilt

For many women, saying "no" elicits an immediate feeling of guilt, regardless of the appropriateness of the refusal. The following situations show you how saying no can be an effective—and guilt-free—process. As you read them, look for the broken record technique as well as others we have mentioned. Imagine yourself in the situations as you read them, and practice feeling good about saying no.

"My car is in the shop"

Carol has taken her car into the shop to be repaired. The mechanic gave her an estimate of $55.00 for the repairs. When she returns to pick up her car, she is told that the repairs come to $110.00. Carol asks to see the shop manager, and tells her/him that the price is much higher than the estimate that she was given, and that she feels the higher charges are not justified. The manager begins a lengthy description of all repairs performed on her car.

Carol listens carefully, and replies that she still believes the charges are much too high. She adds that she will contact the Automotive Repair Board to complain about the charges, and that she doesn't wish to bring her car to this repair shop in the future. The manager consults with the mechanic and upon her/his return, concedes that the mechanic had made an error in the computation, and the charges will be $55.00. Carol pays the charges but resolves to find a more trustworthy repair shop.

"Writer's block"

Kathleen and Karen are students working together on a joint term paper. They are meeting to divide up the writing. Kathleen suggests that Karen do most of the writing, since Karen is a much better writer. Karen says that she feels Kathleen's request is unreasonable, and that the term paper is to be a joint effort. She states further that she would like Kathleen to do her share of the writing. Kathleen continues to explain that she doesn't have Karen's confidence in her writing ability and that she will need the time to study for another class which she is failing. Karen indicates that she understands Kathleen's problem and can sympathize with it, but that she expects Kathleen to share the writing fairly. Karen suggests that they meet weekly to exchange and critique each other's work, and to give each other support until the paper is finished. Kathleen agrees, and they begin to work.

"It's not quite what I want."

Debbie has been shopping for a sturdy bookcase. She enters a department store and asks the salesperson to show her several bookcases. The salesperson shows her many different models, but none of them are quite suitable for Debbie's needs. Debbie tells the salesperson that she doesn't think any of them will work out, and the salesperson takes her to another section of the store where there are several more models. After disassembling one of them to demonstrate how sturdily built it is, the salesperson asks Debbie if she doesn't think it would do. Debbie feels quite empathetic toward the salesperson because of all the time and effort she/he took to show her the bookcases, but she has not found what she wanted. She thanks the salesperson for all the help, and states that the bookcases aren't quite what she had in mind. She leaves the store, glad that she didn't buy something that she really didn't like, despite the salesperson's extra efforts.

"Would you stay with the kids tonight?"

Kay's parents request that she do quite a bit of babysitting for her brothers and sisters. Her parents are very active, and Kay is often asked to babysit four or five nights a week. As a result, Kay is missing out on many social activities with her friends. Kay has tried sulking and moping around the house without any success. She decides to try to openly explain her feelings to her parents and reach some kind of compromise. When she does, her parents are surprised and indignant. Kay repeats her feelings calmly, explaining the situation and emphasizing that she would very much like to participate in some social activities of her own. She adds that she would be willing to babysit once or twice a week, but says that babysitting four or five times a week is really unreasonable. Her parents feel that her solution is a good one and they agree to get another babysitter for other times. Kay feels good about the outcome and does not feel that she has "let her parents down."

"But what about Grandfather?"

Suzanne's 80-year-old grandfather has been bedridden for several months. Suzanne is particularly fond of him, and she often seeks his opinion on matters that are very important to her. Recently, however, he has been demanding to see Suzanne more often and asking her to read to him for several hours at a time. Suzanne wants to comfort her grandfather in whatever ways she can, but his requests are interfering with her other activities. She doesn't want to hurt her grandfather's feelings, but she feels she must find a way to say no to his unreasonable requests. Suzanne tells her grandfather that she would really like to help as much as possible, and explains her other responsibilities. She gently tells him that she doesn't have enough time to comply with all his requests, but that she will do whatever she is able to help her grandfather. Her grandfather says that he understands her situation, and that he is glad she didn't try to "humor" him or treat him condescendingly. They both look forward to future happy visits.

A resource checklist

The first step in protecting your resources and making your strengths work *for* you is identifying what those resources are. Our exercise below will help you to identify what personal strengths *you* have and want to preserve. Check as many as apply to you.

• What do you spend a large part of your time doing?

_____ cooking, laundry

_____ studying, reading

_____ working away from home

_____ driving

_____ attending school

_____ caring for children, family members

_____ pursuing hobby (photography, writing, etc.)

_____ watching TV, movies

_____ entertaining

_____ other _____

• What specific requests are regularly made of you?

_____ driving

_____ doing errands

_____ working overtime

_____ attending meetings, accepting leadership positions

_____ talking with friends, counseling friends

_____ donating time or volunteering for worthy causes

_____ travelling

_____ other _____

• What tasks or situations do your family and friends frequently call on you to help with?

_____ housecleaning

_____ cooking

_____ chauffeuring

_____ watching the children

_____ loaning money

_____ visiting and caring for relatives

_____ other _____

• If you feel proficient in certain areas, do you leave yourself enough time to enjoy "doing your thing"?

Give some thought to these questions and try to identify the resources you have by looking closely at your answers. They will give you an idea of the resources you draw upon often and need to protect.

The assertive woman can say "no" to requests when she is already busy, and she can give herself time to decide what she will do. By exercising these two options, she protects her strengths and prevents them from becoming her liabilities.

VIII. Manipulation and Counter-Manipulation

Women have the same desires as men, but do not have the same right to express them.
—*Jean Jacques Rousseau*

Manipulation involves particularly devious or indirect methods to induce someone to do something, or to behave in a certain manner. It is also common to "manipulate the circumstances" so that a desired result is achieved. The necessary participants of any manipulation are the manipulator and the person being manipulated —or the "set-up operator" and the "victim."

Manipulation is thoroughly discussed by George Bach in *The Intimate Enemy*. According to Bach, the set-up operator's job is to get the victim to *collude*, or go along with, the manipulative actions at the victim's own expense. The experienced set-up operator accomplishes this end through the skillful use of manipulative maneuvers. The manipulator's objective, conscious or unconscious, is to get the victim to do something for her/him without being honest about what she/he wants done, and without taking any responsibility for her/his actions.

Manipulators often believe that they are acting out of loving, caring feelings. The end result of their love, however, is usually painful for those with whom they interact.

"Have a drink"

Iris' husband, George, has been a problem drinker for ten years. He has tried repeatedly to stop drinking, but his attempts are always short-lived. After George has decided to try again to stop drinking, and has attended two meetings of Alcoholics Anonymous, he feels that this time he will really be able to stop drinking.

After a particularly trying week at work, George feels depressed and hopeless. He complains bitterly to his wife Iris about his working conditions and his low mood. In a comforting tone, Iris replies, "Yes, you've really been working too hard recently. Those people don't know how valuable an employee you are! You really have been trying to do so much—not drinking, working late—you can't relax anymore. In fact, that company you work for would make anyone want to drink now and then to preserve their sanity! Maybe just a small glass of wine with me would help you to relax and think things over calmly."

Iris' well-intentioned offer results in painful consequences for George. One glass of wine soon becomes a whole bottle—and one month of progress becomes another unsuccessful attempt to stop drinking. By suggesting that George have a drink to relax, Iris encourages George's self-destructive habit while blaming his drinking on his employer. We may speculate that Iris unconsciously feels threatened by George's progress, and that she wants to keep him dependent on her. By blaming George's drinking on his work tensions, Iris evades her responsibility for giving George a shove "off the wagon." As long as George continues to drink, Iris will feel that she is needed to "help him."

Defining manipulation

Because women have been denied access to direct means to attain their desired goals, they have had to rely on indirect, or manipulative, methods as their primary vehicle for power and control. From childhood, women are taught to "wrap him around her little finger", to "play it cool", or to "play hard to get." It has been considered unfeminine to be anything less than an expert manipulator, especially where personal relationships are concerned. Women are also often passive victims of manipulative actions, particularly when the Compassion Trap is used to manipulate them.

We define manipulation, then, as the conscious or unconscious use of indirect and dishonest means to achieve a desired goal. Still, persistent assertion is sometimes confused with manipulation. Acting assertively in a persistent manner involves using the broken record technique (Chapter VII, "Saying No") to repeat a direct assertive message.

Manipulation can also be persistent and extremely persuasive, but it is characteristically indirect: what is being said is not necessarily what is meant. Persistent assertions are honest and straightforward, and the assertive person will act for her/himself, but will not choose for others. Manipulation is deceptive, and the manipulator is acting through indirect means to get someone to do something. The manipulator will "set it up" to choose for you by making you feel that you have no choice but to do as she/he wishes. If you have been manipulated, you were probably left wondering how you were "conned" into it.

"I'll try to finish everything."

To illustrate this difference, suppose two roommates had planned to do some house cleaning together on a particular evening. Iris is just starting to assemble the vacuum cleaner when Doris says that she has to attend a very important meeting that same evening, and cannot help with the cleaning. Doris suggests that they postpone the cleaning until the following evening. If Iris responds in her usual non-assertive, manipulative manner, the situation will be something like this:

Iris: (sheepishly) "Do you really have to go? I mean, we had planned to do it all tonight."

Doris: (firmly) "Yes, I really should go. I'd hate to miss the meeting, even though we had planned to clean the house. (weakening) You don't mind, do you?"

Iris: (actually minding very much) "Oh *no*, Doris. You go right ahead. I'll just do it all *somehow*." (sounding pained and overwhelmed)

Doris: (feeling guilty) "Well, maybe I could miss the meeting to help you—are you sure we couldn't do it tomorrow night?"

Iris: "No, I really couldn't. I promised to help with voter registration, and you know how important that is. (sounding overburdened) But, you just go on. I'll try to finish everything."

Doris: (feeling even guiltier and colluding with Iris) "No, Iris, I'll stay and help you. It's really too big a job for one person anyway. I'll just skip the meeting."

Iris succeeds in getting Doris to stay home and help her clean by playing on Doris's guilt. Iris felt that it would be too aggressive to state honestly that she wanted Doris to help her. Although she genuinely cares for Doris and didn't want to hurt her, Iris' manipulation is really destructive to honest, assertive communication. In this example, Doris is left feeling angry and resentful toward Iris. If this self-defeating pattern of communication continues, any bond of trust will become seriously weakened, and a broken friendship could be the ultimate result.

"I don't want to do it all myself."

Suppose the same situation were handled assertively by both Iris and Doris. Notice the differences between our manipulative encounter and the use of persistent assertion:

Iris: "I was counting on cleaning the house tonight, Doris, and I'm upset that you've made other plans." (honest, straightforward)

Doris: "I can understand that you're upset, Iris. Cleaning is a big job, and both of us should try to share it. This meeting is really important to me, though, and I want to attend it tonight. Can we get together after the meeting to arrange another time to clean?"

Iris: "Yes, that would make me feel better. But I'm still upset that we can't do it tonight, and I don't want to do it all myself." (takes responsibility for feelings)

Doris: "I really do understand how you feel. It's frustrating to have plans changed at the last minute. The meeting is important to **me**. I really want to go to it. (persistent, honest assertion) I'll be home about nine; so let's talk then and arrange a time that's good for both of us."

Iris: "Okay, I'm glad you understand how I feel. See you later."
In this example, Iris and Doris effectively and assertively communicated with each other. Both women are honest and take responsibility for their feelings, without resorting to indirectly aggressive or manipulative techniques. Their trust, and their friendship, remains strong and intact.

Emotional blackmail

Emotional blackmail, a new and popular concept, is potentially the most powerful kind of manipulative technique. The emotional blackmailer, whether consciously or unconsciously, is an extremely skilled manipulator who coerces a victim into a particular action by playing on the victim's compassion, fear or guilt. Emotional blackmailers, as well as other manipulators, find ideal targets in women who are in the Compassion Trap. Because overly compassionate women place others' wishes and feelings ahead of their own, they are easily manipulated and exploited, and can easily be made to feel guilty for thinking of their own feelings and needs.

Emotional blackmail can only take place under certain conditions. Most commonly, it involves two people who have established a close personal or intimate relationship (mother and daughter; husband and wife; sister and sister; two close friends). Just because you have a close relationship with someone does not mean you will end up as a blackmailer or the victim. But if you tend to be non-assertive as Doris Doormat, or to express your aggression indirectly (Iris) or put down others in order to put yourself up (Agatha), your relationships can be fertile ground for emotional blackmail.

This is how it works: once a close relationship has been established, the blackmailer will interact with the victim in the best, and sometimes the only way she/he knows: through indirect manipulation. The victim is always someone who cares for or loves the blackmailer. The blackmailer always has something the victim wants—usually love or attention in return. Once these conditions are present, the blackmailer can coerce the victim into a particular action (or prevent the victim from doing something) by capitalizing on the victim's emotions. The victims will remain blackmailed as long as they continue to fear the consequences of asserting themselves to get out of the blackmail trap (which usually involves fear of losing the blackmailer's love, etc.). As with other manipulative actions, for the manipulation to be successful, the victim of emotional blackmail must be made to collude with the blackmailer.

The following examples of emotional blackmail illustrate the subtlety of the manipulative process.

"Woman's night out"

Situation: A woman is getting ready to leave for her women's group meeting one evening when her husband says to her: "Well, a 'woman's' night out with the girls is fine. I have my night out, too. But you share our personal intimate secrets with them! I am always the villain. How could you humiliate me like that? You must not value our relationship as much as I do if you are willing to make it common knowledge to all those women. I just don't know how long I can take this. If I leave you, you'll know it's not because I let *you* down."

Result: The woman (victim) decides she'd rather cancel her meeting than feel guilty for causing her husband (blackmailer) so much pain.

A more assertive, honest message from the blackmailer might be: "I'm upset about you going to your meeting because I'm afraid you'll become so independent that you won't need me for anything anymore."

"Letter of recommendation"

Situation: Two close friends are discussing the difficulty of getting a good job in their field. Iris has a lead on a job opening, and has asked April if she would submit a letter of recommendation to the prospective employer. April doesn't feel she can write an informative letter because she has never worked with Iris and knows nothing specific about Iris' skills. Iris pleads with April to write the letter anyway: "Look, we've been friends for a long time. You know me better than anyone. If you were *really* my friend, you'd write the letter. If you really cared, you'd do it."

Result: April (victim) decides to write the letter for Iris (blackmailer) to save the friendship.

A more honest and assertive message from Iris could be: "I'm afraid you won't write the letter for me, but I really want you to write it."

"Don't be too friendly"

Situation: A man and woman are on their way to a party where there will be many mutual friends. As they are driving, the man says, "You know, it would be a good idea if you didn't talk to John too much tonight. I know he's a friend of mine, and I like him, but I worry about what people will think if they see you talking with him. His divorce hasn't been final very long, and if you talk to him alone, it would make people wonder what was wrong between us. And besides, you are wearing a very low-cut dress."

Result: The woman (victim) decides she'll avoid talking with John (collusion) because she certainly wouldn't want to give a poor impression of herself or worry the man (blackmailer) she's with.

A more direct message from the blackmailer might be: "I'm feeling insecure and jealous, because I know other people find you attractive. I'm afraid you might leave me for someone else."

All of us may be tempted to blackmail or manipulate someone close to us at some time. We also can be victims of emotional blackmail. The main thing to remember is that manipulative tactics are destructive for relationships and for you as a person. Learning to recognize and to counteract manipulative attempts will help you to be more assertive and honest in your dealings with others, without the potentially disastrous side effects of manipulation (distrust, resentment).

The Question Trap

Before you can deal effectively with manipulation, you have to be able to recognize it when it happens. Gerald Piaget suggests several effective methods for recognizing and dealing with manipulation. One favorite technique used by manipulators is the manipulative use of questions. This can be a strong manipulative weapon against women, because we have been taught that we not only must answer all questions asked of us, but we must also answer immediately and truthfully. Manipulators rely on that pre-conditioning when they use questions dishonestly.

One of Gerald Piaget's examples of a manipulative "trap" question is a "why" question. Although "why" questions can also be used appropriately, without hidden motives, more frequently "why" questions seem to be not questions at all, but disguised statements or accusations. Putting a statement in a "why" question form evades responsibility for the statement. Typically the person asking the "why" question already knows the answer, but is really trying to corner you or to start an argument. Other questions can be used in the same deceptive way as the chart indicates:

"Why Question	Really Means
"Why were you so late?"	"I don't think you should have been so late."
"Why can't you keep your room clean?"	"I don't think you should leave your room so messy."
"Why were you so rude with me?"	"I don't think you should be so rude with me."

Additional Deceptive Questions	Really Means
(A parent, knowing the daughter/ son has *not* taken the garbage out yet):	
"Have you taken out the garbage?"	"I want you to take out the garbage."
(A spouse, knowing the other has *not* called the restaurant to make dinner reservations):	
"Have you called the restaurant for reservations?"	"I want you to call the restaurant to make dinner reservations."

The peril in using questions manipulatively is that you will teach others not to trust your questions, and they will react badly to your future questions. If asked a manipulative "why" question, the assertive woman makes it her policy to *not* answer. She knows she doesn't *have* to answer any question she doesn't want to. An especially effective reply to the "why" question or deceptive question is, "Why do you ask?" This will usually cause the questioner to say what she/he really means. Try to eliminate deceptive "why" questions from your vocabulary. There is more to be gained by being straightforward and taking responsibility for your feelings.

Another manipulative approach described by Piaget is the use of particular phrases that actually mean the opposite of what they sound. These, again, are designed to allow the manipulator to avoid taking responsibility. Some common examples of these "red flag" words and phrases are:

Red Flag Words	Often Really Means
"I don't know."	"I really do know but I don't want to take responsibility for it."
"I can't."	"I won't."
"I'll try."	"I won't."
"I should."	"I don't want to."

When you hear these phrases, mentally send up a little red flag to signal you to be prepared for a deceptive statement. Unless you really mean it, avoid using these phrases yourself.

A third manipulative tactic Piaget calls "word loading." Only people who know you fairly well can use this one to manipulate you, because it depends on being able to identify your vulnerabilities, or "buttons". The manipulator will try to get to you by pushing your button. If you are sensitive about your weight, a manipulator can push your "weight" button by callling you a "fat slob." If you are sensitive about your intellect, the manipulator can push your "intelligence" button by calling you "ignorant" or "brainy." If you hate to disappoint anyone, a manipulator can tell you that you have "disappointed her/him" and push your button. The best protection against this kind of manipulation is to be able to identify what your "buttons" are. Then you can practice "deactivating your buttons" by learning not to react when someone tries to manipulate you by pushing your buttons, so that a would-be manipulator can't catch you off balance.

Deactivate your buttons

Together with a friend, make up your button list. Exchange lists, and read each vulnerability aloud as realistically as possible, while you practice not responding to them. Use this check list to identify the buttons that apply to you and include some of your own.

Button list

_____ Being told I disappoint someone.

_____ Being told I am unreliable, untrustworthy, etc.

_____ Being told that I smoke too much, bite my nails, or some other bad habit.

_____ Being told that I am overweight, underweight, etc.

_____ Being teased about my freckles, new hair style, style of dress, etc.

_____ Being ridiculed or teased about my sex, home town, accent, race, or income bracket.

_____ Other items that make you feel vulnerable: _____
_____

Not responding will involve controlling your facial muscles so you don't automatically smile or laugh nervously. It will include controlling whatever anxiety responses you usually feel when someone has pushed your button.

Practice relaxation as you listen to your friend trying to push your buttons. What you are doing is exercising your choice not to react, and giving yourself a feeling of control. When you can go through all of your buttons on your lists without reacting with undue anxiety or hostility, you will have made it difficult for the buttons to control you, and you can thwart a button-pusher's attempts to manipulate you. This isn't as easy as it sounds. You may be unable to deactivate your buttons alone. Consulting a professional counselor or therapist can provide you with the extra support you may need.

Counter-Manipulation

There are two major counter-manipulation techniques you can use when you feel you are being "set up" as a victim. By using counter-manipulation, you refuse to be manipulated and you promote assertive communication. The first technique is to respond to what is said, not to what you know is meant. In our first example with the two roommates, April could have responded only to what Iris actually *said*, instead of responding to what she knew Iris meant:

"You go right ahead."

Iris: (sheepishly) "Do you really have to go? I mean, we had planned to do it all tonight."

April: (firmly) "Yes, I really want to go. I'd hate to miss the meeting even though we had planned to clean the house."

Iris: "Well, you go right ahead. I really don't mind at all. I'll do it all somehow. Really, April, it's fine with me." (meaning that it's *not* fine at all)

April: "That's great, Iris. I'm glad you understand. I'll see you later."

"Fighting fire with fire" as in this example, will not solve the problem, but it will solve the immediate communication problem and keep you from being a victim. Using this counter-manipulation method will also discourage the manipulator from trying to manipulate you again. It is not, however, a permanent solution to the problem.

"Reading between the lines."

The second major counter-manipulation technique can help cut through manipulation to encourage assertive, honest communication. It involves "reading between the lines" and getting the manipulator to be honest about what she/he really wants. Piaget describes three components of this process:

1. *Parroting:* Repeating back exactly what was said to you.
2. *Summarizing:* Verifying what was said to you by summarizing it and asking for acknowledgement.
3. *Reflection:* Reading between the lines: "You seem angry with me."

To demonstrate how you can use these techniques to cut through manipulation, let's go back to our two roommates again. This time, April will be able to get Iris to say what she really means, because she knows how to handle manipulation with the three techniques:

Iris: (sheepishly) "Do you really have to go? I mean, we had planned to do the cleaning tonight."

April: (firmly) "Yes, I really want to go. I'd hate to miss the meeting, even though we had planned to clean house."

Iris: (actually very angry) "Well, I really don't mind. You go on ahead. I'll just try to do it somehow. Really, I don't mind."

April: (parroting) "You don't mind that I'm going to the meeting tonight, Iris?"

Iris: (minding very much) "No, I can understand. (sounding terribly overburdened) You have to go to the meeting, and that's it.

(voice louder) I'll just stay here. I'm pretty tired—I've been busy—but you go ahead."

April: (summarizing) "Are you saying that you don't mind my going to the meeting, Iris? That means you would have to do the cleaning . . ."

Iris: (interrupting) "Right—I don't mind. I can see why you don't want to do the cleaning."

April: (reflection) "You seem angry that I'm going to the meeting instead of helping you clean the house."

Iris: (lying) (voice louder) "Me? Of course not! Go ahead to your meeting."

April: (reflection) (gently) "Iris, you do seem upset to me."

Iris: (beginning to say what she really feels) "Well, I guess I am a little upset."

April: (reflection) "Yes—and I would be, too."

Iris: "You would?"

April: (reflection) "Sure, I'd probably feel deserted and as if you didn't care about helping with the cleaning at all."

Iris: (honest) "Yes, that's really it. I don't want you to leave me with all the cleaning. I guess I'm pretty angry about it."

April: "I'm really glad I know how you feel now. I do have to attend the meeting, though—why don't we get together after it's over and plan a time to do the cleaning together?"

Iris: "Okay. I'd feel better then, and maybe we could figure out some way to plan the cleaning for a good time for both of us—so other things don't get in the way."

April: "That's a great idea. See you in a couple of hours." (supporting Iris for being honest)

This discussion resulted in assertive communication, with both April and Iris feeling good about the decision: April attended her meeting and Iris expressed how she *really* felt.

When you try this technique, keep in mind that it may take a little longer to accomplish than the others, but the results are worth the effort. Remember to keep your voice even and well-modulated. Handling manipulation this way does take some self-control and patience—but if you do that, and learn to use the other counter-manipulation guidelines we've presented, you can be confident that you don't have to consent to being a helpless "victim" of even an experienced "set up operator's" plans to blackmail or manipulate you. You can be an assertive woman.

IX. Asserting Your Sensuality

*"I say get it while you can. Don't you turn
your sweet back on love."*
—Janis Joplin

Volumes have been written on sex and how to go about learning many exotic sexual techniques. Some of these books are very helpful; others are destructive, inaccurate, and sexist. Albert Ellis, an established author and psychologist, has written an excellent book about what's wrong with many of the most popular books on sex, *The Sensuous Person: Critique and Corrections.* Also, Masters and Johnson have done extensive research on sexuality in recent years, which has been extremely helpful in dispelling many sexual myths. We encourage you to look through all of the books on sexuality listed in our bibliography. They will provide you with some insights into your basic sexuality.

Because these resources are quite adequate, we will stay away from the "how-to-do-it" approach and concentrate on the concept of being "sensually assertive." As Marilyn Salzman-Webb suggests in her chapter from *Roles Women Play,* it is time to usher out the era in which "women are to be screwed and not heard."

Being sensually assertive involves not only an appreciation of all your bodily senses but an ability to experience your environment through sight, sound, smell, taste, and touch in a direct, straightforward way. The assertive woman allows nothing to inhibit her from feeling alive, energetic, and sensitive to life. She feels free to go to an art show and experience it in a completely visual way that is unique and personal for her, without feeling compelled to provide intellectual interpretations for those around her or to justify her likes and dislikes. April can be turned on to something she sees regardless of what others think. Similarly, her music, her enjoyment of the sounds of the natural outdoors, babies cooing, her own voice, etc. are all open for her pleasure.

The assertive woman is not shy about her sense of taste. She allows herself to explore different tastes whether they be food, drink, or the tastes of her lover. Also, she's not afraid of how she may taste to her lover. April does not feel obligated to buy products designed to make her taste or smell unlike her own clean, beautiful, natural self. An assertive woman need not live in paranoia about the way she tastes or smells.

Finally, the sensually assertive woman takes full advantage of her sense of touch. She allows herself to compare the softness of her own skin to the softness of a rose petal, or another woman's skin, or of the head of the male penis. April is not inhibited about feeling herself and her environment through her own sense of touch. This naturally extends, of course, into the whole area of sexuality. Being sensually assertive also involves being open, honest, and straightforward about your own sexuality, first of all to yourself, and then to the people with whom you are intimate, allowing yourself the complete experience of all your senses.

We can benefit from an exploration of sexual stereotypes and attitudes that we have all learned as women. They may be barriers that prevent us from being sensually and sexually assertive. As we discuss sensuality, keep in mind that your sexuality can be expressed along with your sensual self. In other words, we are not limiting sensuality to genital sex. We are including the pleasure derived from the use of all your senses, regardless of whether or not there is genital contact.

Sexual stereotypes

However, before you explore the specifics of being sensually assertive, it is necessary to get in touch with some possible resistances that you may have. One problem in asserting your right to sensual pleasure is that not all women can readily accept the premise that making love can actually be pleasurable for them. Historically, women have received conflicting messages about sex:

Sex is good	Sex is bad
When you are married, you can have sex frequently.	Before marriage sex is taboo; be a virgin.
Sex is a good physical release.	Women don't *need* sex.
Sex is power to get what you want, hold out sexual "favors."	Sex is a wife's duty; you don't have to enjoy it.
To be seductive and flirtatious is feminine.	It's the woman's fault if she gets raped; she seduces men.
A good female sex partner can cure a man's impotency.	Male impotency is a woman's fault.
Penis/vagina sex is more fulfilling and right.	Masturbation may lead to lesbianism or reduce your pleasure with a man.
Pregnancy is beautiful and respectable in marriage.	Pregnancy "out-of-wedlock" is ugly and disgraceful.
Sex is enjoyable.	Sex is to be endured.
A woman naturally knows how to be sensuous.	Being non-orgasmic is a woman's fault.
Total submissive, willing, loving service builds the male ego and gratifies the female.	Birth control is a woman's responsibility and/or "problem."
A sexy, seductive appearance is O.K.	Initiating sex is aggressive and immoral.
Use sex to please your lover.	Male impotency is a woman's fault.

Advertising images say you   Extramarital sex is ugly,
should be a sexpot always.   even if you're bored.

Thus, one message says "sex is filthy" and stresses the qualities of being a virgin until you fall in love and get married. The opposite message, supported through the mass media, says that women are supposed to be sexy, seductive, and submissive. So, on the one hand we are told to fight off our sexual feelings and men as well, while on the other hand we're encouraged to be sexpots.

The woman who is conditioned to be dependent and to seek male approval thinks of sensuality in terms of her partner's needs and wants. She may go so far as to be totally ignorant of her own sensual needs. When a woman feels this dependent and inferior, it is no wonder that she often does not enjoy sex. Women are conditioned to compete with one another in attracting the attention of men, which elicits fear and insecurity about their own sensuality. Some women choose to lie or to remain silent about their fears and unhappiness.

Iris may derive some satisfaction out of tricking her partner into thinking that she is really enjoying sex or she may fake orgasms. But, the price she pays for this is heavy—physically and mentally. This dishonesty to one's own needs can lead to deep resentment and can eventually destroy a loving relationship.

As we have mentioned in previous chapters, a traditional role has been prescribed for feminity. Traditionally it has been considered unwomanly to take the initiative in sex regardless of whether or not the man is an experienced lover. Women have been shy and very sensitive about avoiding doing or saying anything that could "crush the man's ego." The *ideal* woman *responds*, while the ideal man is supposedly aggressive.

Therefore, women are taught to always be on guard, to set the limits of what will be allowed to happen. In the process of warding off this "powerful" male sexuality, women are programmed to feel defensive and at times told to enjoy their powerlessness because that too is supposedly a turn-on.

Since many woman exert a great deal of energy being tuned in to men and intuiting the right things to say and do, they rarely have the inclination to explore their own sensuality and sexuality. Somehow men are expected to know all about sex and to take the entire responsibility for the course of sexual activity, though not for the results of unwanted pregnancy! We cannot stress enough the value of mutuality. The sensually assertive woman will share much more of this sexual and sensual responsibility than did the docile doves of the past.

Taking responsibility for oneself is generally agreed to be a quality of maturity. However, taking responsibility for what other people say or do is a trap. Too often women believe that if they had only tried harder they could have prevented something unfortunate from happening.

For example, courts and other institutions foster this type of thinking and collude with women in rape cases by inferring that if the woman hadn't looked so sexy or in some other way led the rapist on, his passions wouldn't have reached the point of no return. How unfair it has been to blame women for inciting uncontrollable passions in men, while at the same time teaching boys that their sex drive is not within their own control. Modern day sex research has disproved this, and has revealed that a woman's sex drive is equal to a man's, and sometimes greater.

Rape becomes an issue of power instead of sexuality, and women need to be aware of the fact that their powerlessness, *not* their sexuality, is much more of an incentive to male attackers. A friend of ours, Alice McGrath, teaches self-defense for women at Ventura College and feels that the best defense a woman can have against rape is an assertive attitude. She is convinced that silence, trembling, pleas, or tears demonstrate to a would-be attacker that she is indeed helpless and therefore subject to whatever the assailant wants.

Last, but not least, the pervasive Compassion Trap also operates as a hindrance to a woman who attempts to become sensually assertive. For example, Ellis describes the psychological plight of the woman who is put in the position of a "villainess" when she does not give in and ease the "suffering" of a man who is sexually aroused. We agree with him that the sensually assertive woman may *choose* to say to herself: "Isn't it too bad that he is thinking me a villainess; but I really am not one, and his thought that I am is silly! I don't *have to* give in and ease his 'suffering'. Instead I can hold out, show him that he doesn't *have to* suffer that much and that he can feel frustrated without also thinking *it is horrible* to feel it."

Know thyself

Specifically, the process of becoming a sensually assertive woman involves the following:

First of all, you must look at yourself to determine who you are as an individual sensual/sexual person. You need to learn what your own unique sensual/sexual responses and patterns are. This first step is very active and may involve an exploration of your own fantasy life. You can learn a great deal from your fantasies and come to a greater acceptance of your sensual/sexual preferences, which can liberate you from a passive, solely responsive sex life.

Knowing your preferences may also include exploration of your body. It is important for *you* to know what feels good for you instead of passively expecting your partner to read your mind. You should not be afraid to explore your own body, its sensations and responses. The most personal and accurate way to learn about your own sensuality/sexuality is through masturbation. This, of course, is a *choice* that you have as a woman. We are not writing a defense of masturbation, but very strongly suggest that you consider how masturbation may assist you in becoming a more sensually assertive woman. Perhaps you have not allowed yourself to consider the knowledge and research about masturbation which is available to you.

Your needs are real

The next step in the process of becoming sensually assertive is being able to see that your sensual/sexual needs and feelings as a woman are as real and legitimate as any other feelings you have. Once you establish the legitimacy of your own sensuality with yourself, you need to be able to express it directly and honestly. You can do this on the verbal as well as the nonverbal level. The important thing is that *you do it*. It's dishonest to pretend to be interested only in giving pleasure or in liking *no more* than what you get by chance!

Along with your honesty of expression, another aspect of becoming more sensually assertive is to allow yourself to open up to various levels of sensual/sexual expression. This means looking at other possibilities besides the standard penis/vagina, man-on-top, male-initiated, orgasm-oriented sexuality. Being assertive means learning that you have various choices and then feeling free to exercise these options.

Exploring your sensual environment

Lastly, the sensually assertive woman begins to appreciate the many influences that shape her sensuality, whether they be biological, socio-political, intellectual, or emotional. To know what factors you can change and want to change and then to learn how to control these factors for yourself can only enhance your ability to become sensually assertive. You can't just do this in your head; it involves full exploration of all your senses; it involves open discussion with others and must be viewed in relationship to your inter-dependency with others. Achieving *mutuality* in a relationship is the final hallmark for those who are assertive, and is a beautiful reward for those who are willing to risk being open, honest, and direct.

Sensual consciousness razors

The following questions are designed to be a beginning toward getting to know yourself—the first step in becoming sensually assertive. Fill in your answers honestly.

Have you ever indulged yourself in looking at a person or a thing that you found beautiful or interesting? _____
_____

How do you feel about smelling the natural body odors of yourself and your lover? _____
_____
_____

Have you ever explored anything besides food with your tongue and let yourself really taste it? _____
_____
_____

Under what circumstances do you let yourself sing out loud?
_____
_____

How do you feel about making sounds or talking during lovemaking? _____

_____

Are there taboo words that you don't dare utter aloud to your lover? _____

_____

Why do you make love?_____

_____

Do you feel guilty when you masturbate? _____

_____

When you have sexual intercourse, do you always expect to have an orgasm?_____If not, where does this leave you and how do you feel? _____

_____

Do you always expect the same level or orgasmic response?

_____

Have you ever experienced sexual or sensual attraction toward another woman? _____
If so, were you able to talk to her about it? _____

_____

What would or did you say to her? _____

_____

_____

If you are already committed to one person, how do you handle your sexual attraction toward others? _____

_____

If there is no lover in your life presently, do you feel worthless?

_____

Does your self-image depend more on what you think and feel about yourself or upon what you believe others feel and think about you? _____

_____

How do you communicate to your lover what you expect in your love making? _____

_____

_____

Do you have fantasies that you would like to actualize?

_____

_____

How do you share these fantasies with your lover?   _____

_____

Who initiates experimentation in your lovemaking? _____

_____

Finding the future androgynous person

This worksheet will help you to explore your own concepts of woman's role, in an exercise we developed for use in our workshops. We use such lists to stimulate discussion by identifying areas of change.

Use the two lists below: in the first, write down as many descriptive words that you can think of that relate to being a woman and/or feminine in the traditional sense. Then, do the same to describe being a man and/or masculine. Next, go through each list crossing out qualities that you feel are antiquated, distasteful, or negative. When you are finished, combine what is left and consider the implications of these characteristics of the future androgynous person. This is most fun to do with another person or in a group in which you must work out a consensus of opinion for each characteristic.

Woman/Feminine	Androgynous	Man/Masculine

Sensual fantasy

In the space provided below write down, in as much detail as possible, your favorite sensual fantasy. Then share this fantasy openly with your sexual partner or someone with whom you feel close. Remember, sensuality includes more than sex. Decide if this fantasy can have any bearing on how you want to relate as a sensually assertive woman.

Exchanging sexual roles

This next exercise involves making a sincere effort toward acting out a role as honestly as you possibly can. Try switching roles for five minutes with your sexual partner, taking on each other's behavior. If one of you is more passive or assertive be sure to emphasize this when you switch. Exchange names, clothes, or any other props that will best help you to re-enact the other person. You can try this on three different levels:

a) centered on a domestic, routine situation you two usually get into around the house.

b) giving each other a massage, taking turns, and being sure to role-play how you see your partner giving the massage.

c) switch roles in your actual love-making situation, including verbal as well as non-verbal actions. This one may take more than five minutes!

After you have tried this role-reversal, discuss with each other how you felt about it, using the following questions as a guide:

Were you surprised at what your partner did or said? _____
_____
_____

How did you "read" certain things? _____
_____
_____

What did you learn that was new? _____
_____
_____

Were you able to laugh with each other about things that appeared humorous? _____
_____

If not, how can you best deal with each other's preferences?
_____
_____
_____

The sensually assertive woman

The assertive woman becomes sensually assertive by getting to know herself better. She experiences herself and her environment freely and joyously through all of her senses—sight, taste, smell, sound, and touch. She explores her sexual attitudes to discover where she may be inhibited by earlier conditioning. She also explores her physical self through techniques that range from reading about female physiology to actually exploring her own body through masturbation and/or taking a look at another woman's body closely and/or looking at herself with mirrors.

Believing that her own sensual/sexual needs and desires are legitimate and are as real as any other feelings she has is another important way for a woman to be sensually assertive. The assertive woman knows that she has options with regard to how she chooses to express her sensuality. Nothing is wrong if she chooses for her own pleasure something that is not destructive to another person.

Finally, the sensually assertive woman explores her environment through her relationship with others. She feels free to discuss sexuality with other women and with men. She strives for mutuality in a sexual relationship; she knows that she and her partner can exchange roles, they can experiment with various levels of passivity or assertiveness in lovemaking. She can do *anything* she wants to do as long as she isn't destructive to herself or her partner. Being open, honest, and direct about your sexual expression will enhance your sensuality much more than any "how-to-do-it" books will.

X. The Anger in You

Twenty-Mile Zone

i was riding in my car
screaming at the night
screaming at the dark
screaming at fright
i wasn't doing nothing
just driving about
screaming at the dark
letting it out
that's all i was doing
just
letting it out

well along comes a motorcycle
very much to my surprise
i said officer was i speeding
i couldn't see his eyes
he said no you weren't speeding
and he felt where his gun was hung
he said lady you were screaming
at the top of your lung
and you were
doing it alone
you were doing it alone
you were screaming in your car
in a twenty-mile zone
you were doing it alone
you were doing it alone
you were screaming

i said i'll roll up all my windows
don't want to disturb the peace
i'm just a creature
who is looking
for a little release
i said
and what's so wrong with screaming
don't you do it at your games
when the quarterback
breaks an elbow
when the boxer beats and maims

but you were
doing it alone
you were doing it alone
you were screaming in your car
in a twenty-mile zone
you were doing it alone
you were doing it alone
you were screaming

i said animals roar
when they feel like
why can't we do that too
instead of screaming
banzai baby
in the war in the human zoo

he said i got to take you in now
follow me right behind
and let's have no more screaming
like you're out of your mind
so he climbed aboard his cycle
and his red-eyed headlight beamed
and his motor started spinning
and his siren screamed

he was doing it alone
he was doing it alone
he was screaming on his bike
in a twenty-mile zone
i was doing it alone
i was doing it alone
i was screaming in my car
in a twenty-mile zone
we were doing it together
we were doing it together
we were screaming at the dark
in a twenty-mile zone
we were doing it together
alone
in a twenty-mile zone

—by Dory Previn

Dory Previn's song poignantly illustrates the taboo that women have endured against overt expression of anger. Why have women lived with their inability to express anger fully and directly? One of the most obvious reasons is that women have been taught that it is not "lady-like" or feminine to show that they are angry. They have been intimidated by the threat of being called "bitchy," "castrating," "nagging," "aggressive," or "masculine."

Women are trained to hold back their negative feelings. The Compassion Trap prevents women from expressing negatives by making women feel terribly guilty for even thinking of expressing anger or displeasure. After all, it is often said that "someone has to keep peace in the family." Guess who that someone is? Women smile sweetly and grit their teeth hoping that no hint of their anger or hostility will be exposed.

Because anger is a powerful emotion, it is difficult to express for many women who already feel a sense of powerlessness. It is frightening for these women to "play around with anger," since they view it almost as a deadly weapon. To them, anger can only lead to violence, and they feel there's enough violence in the world already. Many women accept that little boys and men may exhibit violence because they're naturally more aggressive. They do not see that much violence in men is conditioned, just as passivity in women has been conditioned. Furthermore, an assertive expression of anger has much more potential to *prevent* violence. Research has revealed that frequently domestic violence, including family murders, are caused by people who found it difficult honestly to express their anger. Instead, they have allowed it to build and fester until they lose control of themselves and then strike out over something as trivial as what TV channel to watch.

One of the most important reasons why women find it difficult to express anger assertively is that they have been told *not* to by the environment. No one has said, "Well, it's all right for women to be angry, and here is the way to express it assertively." No one has modeled for women the skills involved in the open expression of anger. Instead, our models have consisted mostly of viewing "game playing," either in our families or from TV and the movies. It is now time that women learn about anger, accept it, and learn to express it as assertive women. Women can no longer deny that very real part of themselves.

In his book, *Anger*, Leo Madow refers to anger as an "energy" or driving force. Madow talks about several forms of anger that you need to be able to recognize. Some are more obviously forms that have been acceptable for women to use.

Other authors, for example George Bach in his book, *The Intimate Enemy*, define anger as an emotional reaction to feeling used or put down. Bach acknowledges that there is a wide range of anger, as well as a wide range of aggression which varies from what he terms "harmless assertion" to hostility and violence. However, by putting assertion and aggression on the same continuum, even though they are at opposite ends, the reader may confuse them or think they are really synonymous. We have found this to be true when people speak about aggression and assertion in our workshops. For this reason, we have found that defining assertion and aggression as two completely different concepts is more clearly and readily understood. Also, we feel that assertion is very positive, so if we put it on a continuum with aggression, as Bach does, it will take on a negative connotation.

We have chosen to discuss anger separately from aggression and demonstrate how anger is a legitimate feeling that may be expressed in either passive, aggressive, indirect, or assertive ways. We have used Madow's categories of anger in the following examples:

Modified anger

"Modified anger" is expressing annoyance or irritation without really admitting that you are feeling angry: "I'm fed up with this job. No, I'm not angry. I'm just sick and tired. That's all."

This type of anger is most often expressed by Doris, who mistakenly thinks that she is being assertive by complaining. Unfortunately, however, she usually complains to the wrong source, as in the following situation:

"Mirror, mirror on the wall . . ."

Doris: "I bought this facial mask to tighten up my pores and clear up my complexion. Instead my face is covered with a rash, and now I look awful. This cream is useless and a total waste of money."

April: "You sound pretty mad about it. Why don't you return it and get your money back?"

Doris: "Oh, I couldn't do that. I'm not really angry I'm just disgusted with my skin problems. I probably should try something else."

Indirect anger

Another form of anger is "indirect anger." This is Iris' forte. She denies angry feelings while attempting to make the other person feel guilty. Here is an example of Iris being angry with her friend in an indirect way:

"Leave me."

John: "I'm going to be leaving now, and won't see you until next week."

Iris: "Of course, I don't mind. You go right ahead and leave. It doesn't bother me. I've been lonely before. I'm just disappointed that you want to leave me at a time like this. But, go right ahead anyway."

It is relevant here to mention how women may express anger indirectly through their sexuality. Sometimes "holding out" sexually is the only way a woman who feels powerless can release her resentment. In a situation where you find yourself holding back sexually, ask yourself why you're feeling distant. Is it because you're angry? What about? Are you frustrated because you did not handle another situation assertively? Also, if you find yourself being "overly sweet" in a situation, look inside yourself to see if you are compensating for some residue of anger that you have not confronted.

Sometimes when Iris is being "overly sweet" or even condescending and partronizing, she is expressing hostility indirectly toward the other person. Frequently, this elicits a reciprocal response that is an indirect expression of anger also.

"Some of my best friends are black"

Iris: "Just because you're black doesn't make any difference to me. I don't even notice that your hair is frizzy and all that stuff. I really like you. You're just like anybody else. It doesn't bother me the way you talk. I'm sure glad you joined our group."

Angela: "I'm really glad you let me into your group. I'll try not to notice that the rest of you are honkies. Some of my soul sisters think your group is racist because of the way you talk to us like we were to be pitied because we don't look and talk like you. But, that doesn't make me angry. I just feel weird and left out sometimes."

Iris may not recognize that Angela and others are repaying Iris for her insults. Iris will not change until she is directly confronted with her put-downs and how they affect others.

Depression

Perhaps one of the most difficult forms of anger for women to recognize *as anger* is "depression." Depression is really anger that you have turned toward yourself after you have become resigned and feel hopeless about a situation. The anger here is most difficult to recognize because you can get so caught up in the whole process of being down. Frequently, Doris is depressed; it is a logical extension of her passivity. Instead of expressing anger, she may get sick with headaches, nervousness, stomach distress, etc. Or, Doris may "accidentally" cut her finger and then go into a rage, because it's "safe" to be angry about that. Another insidious form of taking anger out on yourself is through overeating and feeling depressed as a result of your obesity. This is a vicious circle. By the way, Iris may also overeat as a way to get even with her husband or lover, who gets very upset with her weight.

Does the following example sound familiar?

"Hating football"

Doris: "I don't know why I have these chest pains. I get fatigued from doing nothing—absolutely nothing. I used to be so outgoing before I got married. Now I don't know how I'd live without my husband. Of course, I wish he'd stay home with me instead of going to all those football games. I get so depressed when he leaves me. There's nothing I can do except stay home or go with him. And, I despise football!"

Iris: "If my husband went to football games that often, I'd really get angry. I'd make him want to do something I want to do, or he'd be sorry."

Doris: "Oh, there's really nothing else I'm interested in now that I'm so sick. I just wish he'd understand me."

Violence

Although violence is an overt, direct expression of anger, it usually is an overreaction. For example, Agatha often feels that she can only express her anger by being totally obnoxious, insulting, and possibly physically abusive. You need not get violent to convince most people that you mean business and command their respect. Being assertive usually gets this point across. However, there are occasions when people have become frustrated in their attempts to be assertive when they are not acknowledged for their efforts. If it is very important for them to achieve their goal, they may see violence as their only vehicle and be driven to it. Violence has erupted on individual, social and political levels, and it is unfortunate that this cycle exists. We believe that, as people become more assertive and "up front" with each other, much unnecessary violence against themselves and others will be extinguished.

"Cry rape"

On a personal level, let's look at a situation which engenders so much anger that it can easily result in violence. A friend of Agatha's has been raped. She seeks Agatha out to help her to go to the police. When she and Agatha get to the police station, they are both treated disrespectfully. A police officer asks Agatha's friend what she did to seduce the guy into going after her. Then he insists that she probably enjoyed the sexual contact, or that she may be lying just to get some poor guy into trouble. Of course, this makes both women very angry and upset. Agatha proceeds to call the officer a "sexist, pig cop." She threatens the officer, saying that he probably rapes women whenever he has the chance, that women have no rights when it comes to law enforcement, that all men are pigs and back each other up in doing violence to women. She is ready to spit on him, when he grabs her arm and shakes her. They get into a tussle and Agatha is booked.

In a situation like this, Agatha's anger is controlling her. She has a legitimate reason to be angered by the officer's humiliating remarks and behavior, but her behavior only reinforces his opinion that all women are hysterical.

Assertive anger

It is easy to recognize assertive anger because it is directly stated. However, it is not physically or verbally abusive in its expression. April lets the officer know that she is really angry by stating her feelings honestly and directly. If she chooses, she may even use humor to get her angry feelings across in a way to ease tensions. In a rape situation April may say something like this:

April: "I have accompanied my friend here to the station because she was very upset about going through the trauma of being forcefully raped. We are not here to play a game on anybody. This is not a joke. I feel angry when I see you refusing to take her seriously. She has been humiliated once and there is no need for her to be humiliated again. Therefore, I would appreciate it if you showed her some human kindness and respect."

Recognizing your anger is the first step toward learning how to deal with anger successfully. Once you notice the feeling it will be important to admit it to yourself as real. So many times women deny their anger after they recognize it, because they don't believe they have a valid reason for it. Of course they feel it is not womanly when one is "unreasonable, non-compassionate, or non-understanding." This perspective in which *we* view ourselves can be so deeply conditioned that we rarely think of expressing ourselves differently. Recognizing anger is not just an intellectual exercise. By recognition we mean actually getting in touch with the emotional feeling of anger.

Once you are in touch with your angry feelings, the next step according to Madow is to identify the source of your anger. *Where* is it coming from? It is easy to blame somebody else for your anger either out of guilt or perhaps to save face in an embarrassing situation. Be sure that you identify the real source.

Next, look at *why* you are angry. At times it may be more convenient to get angry over something incidental rather than face the real cause of your anger, which may be a thwarted wish or expectation unfulfilled.

As many women have become aware of their oppression, often as a result of the Women's Movement, they have rightfully realized that they have accumulated years of stored anger. It seems as though it is expected that a woman in this position must go through an "angry phase" in which she is angry a great deal of the time. This phase usually lasts a few months. Eventually it becomes apparent that the reservoir of anger is close to empty, and the woman is seeking another outlet for her energy. This is when she begins to deal with her anger *appropriately* and *realistically*. This last step can be called assertive use of anger. Good judgment needs to be exercised when asserting yourself when you are angry.

Alberti and Emmons in *Your Perfect Right* discuss various situations in which it may be unwise to be assertive. For example, you may be inviting potential adverse situations when the other person interprets your assertiveness as aggression. The other person may engage in backbiting, aggression, temper tantrums, psychosomatic reactions, over-apologizing or revenge. The assertive woman may choose not to assert herself when she is dealing with overly sensitive individuals or if saying something would be redundant. If she is appropriately understanding when another person is having difficulty, she may decide not to assert herself at that moment. But the assertive woman knows the difference between appropriate understanding and the Compassion Trap. Last, she may choose not to assert herself when she realizes that she is in the wrong.

Action exercises

We started out this chapter with Dory Previn screaming on the highway. And now we are going to ask you to do some "screaming" but perhaps in your own home or another comfortable spot. Once you have found a room of your own, get together with a friend or your women's group and try these exercises:

"X-Y-Z-1-2-3"

Sit facing one other person. One of you choose "letters" and one choose "numbers" to shout randomly at each other. Before you begin shouting think of a situation or person that has made you angry and get in touch with those feelings. As soon as you both are ready, begin shouting simultaneously at one another for at least two minutes. Be aware of whether or not you begin with a bang and soon fade, or, if you begin listening and trying to understand what the other person is shouting. This communication frequently happens with women; if they started with letters they suddenly find themselves speaking their partner's numbers. Could this be the Compassion Trap? Practice until you feel that you can stick with your own anger consistently. Another valuable part of this exercise is in allowing you to get used to how to make angry sounds and to desensitize you to fears of hearing these sounds from others.

The silent movie technique

Next, try to get used to allowing your body to express anger non-verbally! In a film on individual assertive training, Michael Serber demonstrated this effective technique. Facing your partner, pretend that you are both in silent movies and that you are trying to communicate to one another how angry you are. Use facial expressions, gestures, and your body in such a way as to convey your angry feelings *without* talking.

Getting into the "talkies"

Now that you have practiced the verbal and non-verbal parts of anger, put them together in this next exercise: Repeat to each other these phrases using good eye contact and body language, and experimenting with your voice in different ranges or levels of anger:
"I feel angry right now."
"I do not like it when you ignore me."
"I am very upset about what you said/did."
"Stop that!"
Make up other phrases too. Give each other honest feedback on how you are coming across to one another.

Emptying the gunnysack

George Bach developed this exercise to try with someone with whom you feel close but with whom you are having trouble voicing your anger. Each of you take some time alone—an hour or so. Write down all the things from the past and in the present that have made you angry with this person. Then choose a time mutually convenient for both of you to get together in order to read your lists to one another. As you read to the other person, precede each complaint or grievance with, "I feel/get angry when . . ." The person receiving the complaint should listen carefully, being aware of defensive feelings or impulses to be aggressive. By agreement, the listener should just acknowledge the complaint with a nod of confirmation or a statement such as, "I hear you." For this exercise it is not recommended that you get into a discussion after each item on your lists. Put stars by the ones you feel are mutually important to discuss at another pre-arranged time. It will be enough just "putting all your cards out on the table" the first time around.

Disarming an angry person

When someone is very angry at you and is screaming and yelling at you, try the following exercise developed by Cotler and Guerra to disarm the anger. First, acknowledge with an assertive message that you definitely hear her/him. You can say, "I hear you," "I know you're angry at me," etc. Often this acknowledgment will calm the person enough to enable you both to discuss the issue. If not, in a calm, assertive manner say something like, "I really want to talk to you, but I cannot talk to you when you're screaming. As soon as you're calm, I will be happy to talk to you."

You can use the "broken record technique" to reiterate this until the person calms down. Then *listen*. However, if the screaming continues, you have the right to leave the situation. You can say that you are leaving until such time that you both can hear each other out. Or, you can just leave! Women are notorious for "hanging in there" in an argument and often feel compelled to hold out until the "bitter end." This is masochistic and totally unnecessary.

Before you try to disarm an angry person in a real life situation, try to role-play this procedure with a friend until you feel sure about what you are doing. Ask for positive feedback and suggestions. Remember it is very important to support one another when dealing with situations that in the past have caused you anxiety and pain.

XI. Humor—"I'm funny; you're sarcastic"

"Give me an honest laughter."
—Walter Scott

Humor can be used to express love, affection, and caring, and to spotlight your "quick wit." It can also be devastating when used as a weapon to stab others in their Achilles heel—where it hurts most. Women have experienced humor largely as its victims. Women have been targets for countless bad jokes—"Did you hear the one about the mother-in-law?"—and we have laughed because we were expected to laugh. As for developing and using our sense of humor, it simply was not part of being a woman. Like anger, humor was not to be displayed freely by the woman who would remain a "lady": passive, reserved, demure, and quiet.

As women begin to exercise their personal power, our use or misuse of humor takes on new importance. We have a choice. We can choose to exercise our senses of humor actively and assertively. We can choose to get out of the Compassion Trap—trying to please others by laughing at their jokes—and to activate our own humor systems as assertive women.

Women find it hard to trust humor—including their own—because it has so frequently been used against them. The misuse of humor has been the standard. Indeed, we have been taught to collude with joke-tellers who really taught us about self-ridicule.

There's the woman who's elected treasurer for an organization, saying she'd be pleased to take on the job as long as the books don't have to balance to the penny; the woman librarian who misplaces the dictionaries; and the everpresent dumb-but-sexy-girl-after-a-man jokes. We have not been exposed to appropriate models to learn to develop and use our sense of humor. We've learned to laugh, yes, but not at what was really very funny to us. Women have been taught to smile through their pain, to grin and bear it. Worse, we were told that this is how it *should* be. And there we are, trapped by our compassion again.

While the tide has turned against many comic portrayals, women are still subject to ridicule both for their supposed traditional traits and for their new liberated attitudes. Media carefully avoid jokes about Poles, Chinese, Blacks and other minorities, about the handicapped or the poor or the downtrodden, but women are fair game for cartoonists and comics, television writers and comedians.

For example, we have all heard jokes like the following, which are "funny" at the expense of women:

- "Who was that woman I saw you with last night?
  "That was no woman, that was my wife!"
- Happiness is . . . discovering at the kindergarten pageant that when your son said his teacher was 42, he didn't mean her age.
- "You gave your mother-in-law a plant for her birthday?"
  "Yeah, poison ivy."
- "Those women libbers are burning their bras again."
  "Once you see them you would think they'd be padding them instead."
- "Look at that fender; were you in a wreck, Joe?"
  "No, this is my wife's car. You should see our garage door!"
- "Honey, we never seem to have any more conversations together."
  "O.K., so lie down and I'll talk to you."

As women begin to express their anger openly and assertively, they will find that they no longer have to laugh at others' unfunny jokes. They have the freedom to get angry about it. They have the opportunity to develop and to use their own sense of humor, and to refuse to be passive victims of the misuse of humor.

Sarcastic humor

Using humor assertively requires some practice, and involves knowing the difference between its use and abuse. Sarcasm, considered a form of humor, is a powerful tool that can be particularly hostile, and is usually safest in the hands of experienced comedians such as Don Rickles or Harrison and Tyler (the female comedians, not the politicians). When you are confronted with a sarcastic comment, you probably sense anger and hostility passing for "humor."

Sarcasm and caustic wit are Iris' favorites in the name of "being funny." She is, of course, really very hostile and is attempting to upset you with her remarks. Iris may remark to a neighbor who was late for a morning meeting: "Late again, Ethel? You better cut out all that late-night drinking!"—or to an overweight friend who is struggling with a diet—"Sure, Mary, have some cake—you are looking a little underweight today." Obviously, Iris uses "humor" as a vehicle for her insults and hostilities. As a general rule, avoid using sarcasm and "humorous insults" to express your anger. It is better expressed assertively, directly and honestly.

The "Achilles Heel" humorist uses humor to attack others where it hurts most, where they are the most vulnerable. If you have been a victim of this kind of attack, you have felt that others were laughing *at* you.

Consider how April may handle herself with the Achilles Heel humorist in the following situation:

"Starting a revolution?"

Achilles: "Oh, there she is, the Woman's Libber (ha ha)—what are you going to do today—start a revolution or something?"

April: "Yes—I'm starting a revolution, and I'll start with you."

This style of "humor" is directed at a personal characteristic, habit or favorite pasttime of the victim. To the victim, of course, it is not funny at all. April responds to an Achilles Heel attack effectively with a quick retort, or by stating that she doesn't feel that it is very funny to her, and she would like the attacker to stop. If you don't feel as confident with your "comebacks" as you do with telling the attacker to stop, give it a little practice. Review the exercises in

Chapter VI, "Compliments, Criticism and Rejection," particularly the ones that involve creating "comebacks" and responses to put-downs. You don't have to make a witty remark at all if you don't want to. Directly expressing your annoyance is equally effective in stopping an Achilles Heel attacker. The important thing to remember is to *act*, not to become the passive victim by not saying or doing anything.

Teasing

Teasing is another common form of expressing humor by "poking fun" at someone. Sometimes the use of subtle affectionate teasing can be beneficial to help someone overcome anxiety, as George Bach points out in *The Intimate Enemy*. Usually, however, teasing serves to alienate others instead of relaxing them. Taken to its extreme, teasing can be a form of attack used by the Achilles Heel humorist. At this point, teasing isn't funny; it is an expression of aggression rather than affection. Bach describes the strategy of teasing as knowing the vulnerable area of the victim, something that the victim doesn't want displayed to anyone, and then bringing some incident in this area to the attention of others. Consider the following situation, for example:

"Violets are red, roses are blue . . ."

April is enrolled in a poetry class. Agatha has persuaded April to let her read some of her poems. Agatha thinks that April's poems are the funniest things she's ever read, and asks April if she has considered doing comedy writing. Another friend, Iris, enters the room and Agatha reads some poems aloud and asks her if she didn't think April's poems are absolutely hysterical. Iris joins Agatha in laughing at April's work. April had been spending a good deal of time with her poetry, and she is hurt and angered by Agatha's "teasing." Agatha and Iris have alienated April with their "humor."

April has the option to "put up" with their teasing or to demand that it stop: "Come on, cut it out. I don't like to be teased about that."

If April chooses to assert herself and ask that the teasing stop, she will likely be teased a little more, along with being asked,

"What's wrong with you, can't you take a joke?" She can respond with the same request again, using the broken record technique. This should be enough to stop her friends' unfair teasing.

We suggest that you review your use of teasing. Is it affectionate or aggressive and alienating? How have you felt when you've been teased to the point that it's not funny anymore? Try to be aware of how you use teasing as a form of humor, and beware of launching aggressive attacks of teasing. The best rule to follow is to tease sparingly and affectionately. When you tease in that way, you are using humor assertively and lovingly.

Humor—A weapon against yourself

As you grow to understand the importance of the labels you attach to your behavior, you will be more aware of how women have also used humor against themselves in the form of "humorous" self labels: Doris says, "I forgot my checkbook—isn't that just like a woman?" or "You know how I am—I'm just *lost* without my husband" (ha ha). In the guise of gentle humor, Doris perpetuates countless stereotypes. She has made herself the target of "humor" that is not funny at all.

We are not suggesting that being an assertive woman means that you must be humorless, or that you cannot "laugh at yourself" every once in a while. But you can begin to use humor assertively by deciding not to use it as a weapon against yourself or others.

Happily, you can learn to use humor actively and assertively to express yourself uniquely and positively with no residue of anger or negative feelings. Giving yourself permission to *respond* to humorous situations, to laugh at things that make you want to laugh, is the other component of assertive humor. How do you respond to situations you find humorous?

Doris doesn't respond with spontaneous laughter. She waits to see how others respond, and then takes her cues from them. If the laugh, she will join in, but she is careful to stop laughing before everyone else does, so she isn't "caught" laughing too much. Doris may also not laugh at all, fearing rejection if she does laugh. She may also feel guilty because she is enjoying herself.

Agatha, by contrast, laughs uproariously with little provocation. Agatha has to laugh the loudest and the longest. It gives her a chance to "steal the show" and call attention to herself, but other people find her laughter irritating and annoying.

Iris, like Doris, may laugh to hide nervousness or insecurity, but often her laughter is subtle and a thin mask for her hostility.

April will laugh when she finds humor in a particular situation. She won't use her laughter to dominate others, and she doesn't feel guilty or anxious about laughing at something that is funny to her. She is aware of others' feelings and rights, and she will not "laugh in someone's face."

Role imitation

Nena and George O'Neill in *Open Marriage* suggest an exercise for couples that involves the use of humor called "role imitation." By imitating each other, husbands and wives, friends and roommates can hold up a mirror to one another's actions, making each other more aware of unconscious habits. When this is done without malice and with good humor, it can be a "game" that allows you to tell someone else things that you might not otherwise be able to bring up. For example, April and her roommate Iris are sitting in the living room, kidding and joking with each other. Iris begins to imitate the way April acts when Iris has been using the telephone for a while. She mimics the way April paces around the room, clears her throat, and rattles pots and pans in the kitchen in an effort to get Iris off the phone. April, laughing at this humorous critique, then imitates the way Iris interrupts her when she's trying to concentrate on something. She duplicates Iris' questions and manner of delivery exactly "Where's the detergent?" "Sorry to bother you, but how do you work this faucet?"

The result of this technique of imitation is usually disbelief: "Do I really do that?" This humorous approach is certainly better than angrily exploding at someone. When small irritations are pointed out in this way, people won't usually feel they have been attacked. The O'Neills caution that this exercise should be attempted when both people are in the mood for it, and not used by one person in an effort to start a fight. That would be an example of Achilles Heel humor. Try this exercise with whole families and children, also. It can be an assertive way to use humor.

Express your humor

To express your sense of humor assertively, you must first accept the idea that it's OK to try expressing it.

• Doris Doormat would remain passive and would not risk sharing something she found funny with anyone. She fears rejection and needs approval: "What if they don't think it's funny?" She may also feel anxious and guilty about finding humor in a serious situation, and will not joke about it.

• Iris uses humor as a vehicle for her insults and hostilities. She often is an Achilles Heel humorist, who uses humor to attack others where is hurts the most. Sometimes she uses humor to put herself down, to bait the Compassion Trap for others.

• Agatha Aggressive, on the other hand, is a regular comedian —she uses humor aggressively, whenever she possibly can. Those around her try to avoid her as often as possible. They feel that, to Agatha everything is a joke, and their own interests will not get serious attention from her.

• April Assertive knows that it's OK to express her sense of humor. She can say something that is funny to her without feeling unduly anxious or guilty, and without fear of rejection. April knows that some people will laugh and others won't, but exercising her right to say something she thinks is funny without harming others is most important to her.

The assertive woman actively expresses her sense of humor by saying whatever is funny to *her*. Actively expressing your sense of humor means saying whatever is funny to *you*, so long as you are not being injurious to yourself or to someone else. It doesn't matter if someone else doesn't think it's quite as funny as you do, or if you say it in a serious conversation or situation.

To respond assertively to something that you find humorous is to laugh, or smile, or chuckle about it. The important thing to remember is to express your humor, honestly and spontaneously, without feeling guilty or anxious about it, and without aggressively "taking over" every humorous situation.

As an assertive woman, go ahead and express your unique sense of humor—as long as you remember it can be a lethal weapon. Part of being assertive is asserting your sense of humor—it isn't always serious work, but it may take some practice.

XII. Children

"Children are educated by what the grown-up is and not by his talk."
—*Carl A. Jung,*
Psychological Reflections

When you are in the midst of cleaning up spilled milk, officiating over which child gets to watch her/his favorite TV program, bandaging scraped knees, getting youngsters dressed and undressed, into bed and out of bed—acting assertively with them may well be the last thing on your list of things to accomplish. But if you often feel put upon by your or other's children, you may have brought it on yourself by not acting assertively with them and by not allowing them to learn to act assertively themselves.

Remember when you were a child? The unkind nicknames, the neighborhood bully, everyone older or taller telling you what you could or couldn't do? If you were subject to any of that, chances are the only ways you could handle the situation were to leave the field, manipulate the circumstances, or try to wear others down until they gave in. You learned to say "yes" to parental demands in order to get them "off your back," but you really meant "no."

Because children do not have equal power with adults, they may become masters of deception and other manipulative ploys in an effort to exercise some control themselves. And powerful weaponry it is: children have the ability totally to disarm a parent or adult by shaming them and by playing on their vulnerabilities.

Although children can use this kind of self-defense, they generally operate at a disadvantage. Children can rarely correct adults or restrict adults' movements the way adults can restrict children's. George Bach, in *The Intimate Enemy*, outlines in detail the various ways children "fight back," and the relationships that develop between parent and child when communication is mismanaged, particularly in conflict situations. There are several such resources for you to draw upon as you begin to assert yourself in more subtle and difficult situations with others.

We have emphasized that as you become more assertive, you will experience the rewards that go along with it. One of those rewards is seeing those around you become more assertive also. As an assertive woman, you are a "model" for others. Your children, through watching you, can learn how to be independent people and go on to become models for families of their own.

Children, of course, also watch and learn from you when you act non-assertively or are aggressive. They will learn those behaviors as well. This can have unpleasant results for you, as it could for Iris Indirect or Agatha. Iris' children may learn from her example how to be expert manipulators. Agatha's children may adopt her loud, bossy, and bullying ways to get what they want. And Doris' children may learn to be helpless and passive.

Fortunately, children succeed very well in learning to be assertive—and they can learn most of it from you. They will receive the same benefits when they assert themselves as you do when you assert yourself: a feeling of personal worth, strength, and independence.

Your child's assertiveness—a checklist

Acting assertively with children and modeling assertive behavior for them requires some attention to the ways you behave with them now. Briefly review the previous chapters and exercises in this book. Begin by answering the following questions:

• Do you feel they can apply to your child also: Which ones? _____

_____

• Who has more personal rights, you or your child? _____

_____

• What particular rights or privileges do you have that your child doesn't have? _____

_____

• How does your behavior with your children differ from your behavior with adults? _____

_____

• Does your child know what you expect from her/him? In what situations? _____

_____

What attitudes are you teaching your child? Answer the following questions (True or False).

True False

____ ____ Children should be seen and not heard.
____ ____ I spend a good deal of time doing things for my child.
____ ____ I am frequently angry with my child's behavior.
____ ____ My child needs to be protected.
____ ____ My child can make many decisions with my guidance.
____ ____ I encourage my child to do things "for your own good."
____ ____ I feel that my child takes me for granted.
____ ____ My child depends on me for everything.
____ ____ I encourage my child to be independent.
____ ____ I respect my child's feelings and opinions.

Your answers to these questions can help you to see how you usually treat your child. Generally, you may find that in some situations, you treat your child as a "kid." Your behavior in these situations is probably quite different than your behavior with adults. At other times, you probably see your child as a person, although someone with perhaps less personal power than you have. The first step in learning to behave assertively with your child is to recognize her/him as someone with certain personal rights. It is true that you do have to make some decisions for your child's own welfare, but you can also help a child to be assertive and to stand up for herself/himself.

Start by observing what your child actually does and what you *expect* her/him to do. Usually this means distinguishing between appropriate child-as-child behaviors and child-as-adult behaviors.

In some situations, do you expect your child to behave as you would rather than as a child? Although you probably wouldn't play in the mud, your child may, and to expect otherwise is probably unrealistic. If you provide your child with spending money or an allowance, it may also be unrealistic to expect her/him to spend the money (or save it) as you would. Part of helping your child to be assertive, then, is to try to avoid expecting her/him to function as an adult in all situations. You can then provide support and guidance when it is needed and allow the child to tackle other situations independently.

Acting assertively with your children means clearly communicating what you want for them and/or expect from them, and giving them the opportunity to discuss it with you. Accomplishing that will mean that you do not act as the "dictator" or manipulator, or act without recognizing and acknowledging your child's feelings and wishes.

"The Rock Concert"

Situation: Your 13-year-old daughter, Cindy, wants to go to a rock concert in a city 25 miles away. It is a week night, and Cindy has school the next day. Several of her friends are going, and one of the parents will drive. You don't want Cindy to go to the concert on a week night, and you are also uncomfortable with the 25-mile distance. Which approach would you be likely to take?

Passive. After listening to her daughter's pleas to go to the concert, *Doris* says: "Oh, I don't know, Cindy. Who is going to the concert and who is performing?

Cindy: "All of my friends are going, and there will be lots of bands there—I can't remember all of them. Mom, can I go to the concert or not?"

Doris: "Well, I don't know; why don't you ask your father?"

Aggressive. Before Cindy is halfway through her request, Agatha interrupts:

Agatha: "Are you crazy? Going to a silly concert on a school night? What's gotten into you?"

Cindy: "But, Mom—"

Agatha: "No *buts* about it! Absolutely not! And don't talk back to me like that. If you keep making these ridiculous requests—a girl of your age—I'll take away your allowance for a week!"

Cindy: "Mom, you didn't even let me explain—"

Agatha: "I said forget it. Don't you argue with me, young lady. You're not going to be there with all those bad influences."

Indirectly Aggressive. *Iris* listens to Cindy's request attentively, and then says:

Iris: "Cindy, you disappoint me. I thought you had better sense. No, you can't go tonight. It's really for your own good. I'm older and I know about the world."

Cindy: "But, Mom, everyone's going. It will be fun."

Iris: "When you're older, you'll see that I'm doing you a favor. It's only that I care about you. Those other parents must not care at all to let their children go. I wish someone cared more about me when I was a child. You'll be a better person for it, Cindy."

Assertive. April listens to Cindy's request attentively, and then replies:

April: "Well, Cindy, it does sound like a good concert, and I can see you really want to go, but I'll have to say 'no' this time."

Cindy: "But Mom, all my friends are going! I'll be the only one who will miss it!"

April: "I know several of your friends are going. But tonight is a school night and you have to get up early tomorrow morning. I really have to say no. I'm glad you asked me, Cindy, and I think concerts are fun to go to. Going to a Friday or Saturday night concert would be OK but I must say 'no' under these circumstances."

In this situation, Doris is tentative with her "no," and ultimately passes the decision on to someone else. Doris is not specific about what she expects her daughter to do. She is more concerned about not displeasing her daughter by saying "no." On the other hand, Agatha does not allow Cindy to finish her request or to state her feelings. Agatha gives excessive orders and commands and behaves like a dictator. In this case, Agatha's daughter has only the right to obey her mother's commands. The manipulative Iris uses an indirect approach with her daughter, by making Cindy feel guilty for making her request. It is difficult to see how this experience would make her daughter "a better person," as Iris says; Iris is not straightforward with her "no." However, April is able to handle this situation assertively and communicate to her daughter that she has the right to disagree and to bring the subject up again later. April doesn't precede her "no" with a moral lecture, nor does she overload Cindy with commands and punishments. By her response April encourages assertive communication.

Generally, you should approach acting assertively with children in the same way you do with adults. We have labeled two particular communication traps to beware of when interacting with children: as the "Aggression Trap" and the "Slavery Trap." Each could prevent you from acting assertively with your children.

The Aggression Trap

This trap short-circuits assertive communication because you find yourself practically forced into "exploding" at your children. It generally occurs when you have put off asserting yourself with your children, hoping that the situation would change of its own accord, without your intervention.

"It's marijuana"

Situation: You have suspected that your 14-year-old son, Gordon, has been experimenting with marijuana. You haven't mentioned anything to him about it, hoping that it was only temporary. You are hanging up Gordon's jacket one day when a marijuana cirgarette falls out of the jacket pocket. You approach Gordon, waving the cigarette in front of him: "I knew it! I knew it all along! Next thing I know you'll be hooked on something stronger! Have you lost your mind? What are you trying to do, land in jail? I can't believe you'd do anything so stupid! Can't you see how dumb you've been? You'll probably turn into a real addict!"

If you have been in the Aggression Trap, you know you are left feeling shaky and angry at yourself for exploding. The trap can be avoided by dealing honestly and assertively with your problems when they appear. Hoping the situation will improve or ignoring it can build you up for a headlong plunge into an aggressive, irrational encounter. Many parents behave this way routinely with their children. In doing so, they risk blocking all meaningful communication.

An assertive approach with the same situation would occur as soon as you sense there might be a problem or something to talk about. It might go like this: "Gordon, I have something I want to talk to you about that's been bothering me lately. I think you might be smoking marijuana, and I'm concerned about it. I'd like to hear your side of it."

The assertive parent acknowledges her/her child's feelings and wishes, and then states what she/he would like the child to do.

"You may decide to continue smoking marijuana, even though you're aware of the risks involved. But I don't want you to have it here in the house, and I don't want you to smoke it here, either. You will have to accept the responsibility and the risks of using it. I can't support you in this situation, and I'd really prefer you didn't use it at all."

The Slavery Trap

When you perform an excessive number of tasks for your children, most of them unnecessary, you are in the Slavery Trap. This trap encourages your children to be too dependent on you. Your children are not likely to learn assertive behaviors and independence when you are a model for this pattern of behavior.

For example, a typical morning finds Doris awakening her children for school, bathing and dressing them, preparing breakfast, packing lunches, and driving them to school (only a few blocks away). Realistically, all of these tasks could be performed independently by the children. Doris is actually doing her children a disservice by not allowing them to manage their own behaviors. Because they have learned to be too dependent, they will have great difficulties standing up for themselves when necessary. Parents permit the Slavery Trap at the cost of their child's independence and assertiveness—a high price to pay. Doris may also pay a high price as a result of the Slavery Trap. She may grow to resent her children, find that she has little time for herself, and worst of all, once her children are grown, she may realize that her "slavery" was more of a burden to her children than a benefit to them.

Inheriting the Compassion Trap

Parents can pull their children into the Compassion Trap with them by making the children responsible for taking care of their parents' needs. This happens frequently with single parents, who often refer to their child as the new "man" or "woman" of the house, with additional responsibilities to the parent. The children may resent being placed in this position, but usually do not complain too much because they would feel guilty for saying anything.

A parent who feels helpless can engender a feeling of responsibility in a child by forcing her/him to make decisions or take on adult responsibilities prematurely. The parent may foster guilt in the child as well as excessive compassion. The parents' message is "Care about your parent! Don't you feel sorry for me?"

You know your child is in the Compassion Trap if she/he is more than frequently saying: "Don't worry, I'll take care of you; I'll do that for you, you're too sick; I won't leave you alone." It is understandable that children in the Compassion Trap experience tremendous guilt feelings for pursuing their own interests. They may also develop an attitude of parental over-protectiveness that can stay with them well into adulthood, something they pass on to their own children.

Forcing your children to be your "parent" deprives them of their right to choose how they will live. Since the average lifespan is 75 years, it isn't too much to allow children to be children for 10 or so years.

In the land of giants

How you assert yourself with children is also important. Emphasizing the physical components of assertive behavior is equally important when you are asserting yourself with your children.

Getting your child's attention so you can talk with her/him is an important part of acting assertively with children. Combining several techniques is most effective, particularly with younger children.

• Since you are much taller than your child, try bending down so that your child looks down at *you* while you are talking. You can also do this by squatting or sitting on the floor while your child is seated. The goal is to avoid looking like a giant to your child, and to help maintain eye contact, just as you would with an adult.

• Touching your child—holding her/his hand, touching her/his knee while you are talking will help keep your child's attention directed toward you.

• You can also get your child's attention by saying, "Listen to what I'm going to say, because it's important." Be sure that your voice is loud enough to be heard, but don't unduly raise your voice. Experiment with your voice volume to find what works best for you. Sometimes keeping your voice lower than normal is an effective attention-getter also.

Combining these techniques also serves to give you the appearance of being an "equal" who will talk *with*, not yell *at*, your child.

Roleplaying with your child

We believe that the best way to teach your children to be assertive is to act assertively yourself. Since you cannot be with your children all the time, you can also teach your children to be assertive by giving them specific instructions, and by "role-playing" with them. Suppose your seven-year-old son has a friend who likes to play with matches. Your son tells you that his friend had been playing with the matches one day after school, and that he wanted your son to play with them, too. Your son doesn't want his friend to play with the matches, but he doesn't know how to tell him that. You decide to help your son handle the situation assertively. To do it, you pretend to be your son's friend, and have your son practice telling you assertively he doesn't want you to play with the matches ("Tommy, I don't want you to play with matches while you're with me."). You can give your son encouragement and support for being appropriately assertive ("That's right!" "That's good.") and then add any suggestions for improvement ("Try saying that again in a louder voice."). You may also switch roles: you pretend to be your son, and your son takes the role of his friend. You can use role-playing with your child very successfully to teach assertion. Young children particularly like this approach because of its "game" nature. The advantage of this approach is that by watching you, your son can see firsthand how he should act. Then switch back again, and have your son practice once more before trying it for real with his friend.

Another effective approach to encourage assertive behavior patterns with your children is to aggree on a "contract." If both parent and child abide by the terms of the contract, aggressive outbursts and mismanaged communication can be considerably reduced.

A contract has the advantage of clearly specifying what is expected of both parties. Also specified is what each party will receive for keeping up her/his part of the agreement. Some families prefer to have loosely structured, verbal agreements, while others may choose to write down the terms of the contract. A sample contract is shown below:

Child	**Parents**
Complete homework assignments	Allow child to watch TV after homework.
Does home chores.	Provide allowance.
Tells parents where she/he is going, when she/he will be back.	Avoid "nagging."
Does not scatter clothes, possessions around house.	Allow child to keep her/his room in any condition she/he wants. Room is the child's personal territory.

Contractual agreements work well for some families, and others prefer not to use them at all. The choice is up to you and your children. If you do decide to try a contract, remember the importance of following through with the terms.

It is hard work being a parent, and volumes have been written to teach parents about children and their behavior. There are several good books available to help you interact assertively with children. We recommend *Parents are Teachers*, by Wesley C. Becker, *Families*, by Gerald R. Patterson, and *Living with Children*, by Gerald R. Patterson and M. Elizabeth Gullion. All are listed in the *Bibliography*.

We hope you will include children among the people with whom you will behave assertively. If you do, you will find that you feel less put down by their demands, and that they will behave less manipulatively with you. You will be giving them something they can rely on all their lives—a sense of personal worth, strength, and independence.

The following exercises will help assertive parents (and those who are developing assertiveness) to help children to grow toward becoming mature, assertive adults.

"King and Queen" exercise

Our exercise works best with a group of children (at least four and at most ten) approximately seven to ten years old. We designed this exercise to teach children how to give and receive compliments assertively, one of the first steps in learning to be assertive.

The girls and boys in the group take turns being the King or Queen, sitting on the "throne" (a chair placed in the room). The other children and the adult group leader sit in front of the King or Queen as his/her "subjects." The King or Queen calls on the subjects individually, and each comes to the throne bearing a "gift" in the form of a sincere compliment for the King or Queen. The children are encouraged to let their imaginations run, and to imagine that the King or Queen is wearing a royal robe, a jeweled crown, and is holding a sceptre. As subjects, the children can bow down in front of the throne and present their "gift," saying, "Queen Susie, I have brought you this compliment: you are fun to be with." The children are required to make eye contact with the King or Queen when they are bestowing their compliments. The King or Queen must acknowledge the compliment in some way, e.g. "Thank you," "I agree with you," etc.

The rest of the subjects and the group leader monitor the sincerity of the compliments, either by cheering, or saying "that's good," or by giving good-natured "boo's." The children are encouraged to give personal, rather than superficial, compliments. If the compliment is judged by the subjects and adult to be personal ("I like the way you haven't been hitting everyone lately."), the subject receives a reward (fruit, small toy, etc.). If the compliment was thought to be superficial or false flattery ("You're wearing green—that's my favorite color."), the child is encouraged to try again.

The children will lend a great deal of support to each other in this exercise and will offer to help each other out, particularly when a child is having difficulty. This game is really an enjoyable one for children to try.

"A child's perspective" exercise

This exercise, recommended by Virginia Satir in her book, *Peoplemaking*, is intended for two adults (*A* and *B*) to do together. The purpose is to help you to be aware of a child's perspective toward the rest of the world, especially toward adults. *A* stands, while *B* sits on the floor directly in front of *A*.

Carry on a brief two-minute conversation in this position; then discuss how it felt.

Switch positions, carry on another two-minute conversation, and discuss how you felt.

How did your body feel? When you were straining to look up to talk did your neck, shoulders, back and eyes begin to ache? When you were standing did you have to strain to look down? When you talk to your child, try to squat so you are at eye-level as much as possible. It will save both of you some strain, and help to increase your communication.

"The Giant"

Virginia Satir suggests a variation of the above exercise. Assume the same position as in the previous exercise, with one adult standing and one sitting directly in front of the stander. The sitter should just look up and describe what she/he sees: A giant with big feet and enormous arms, perhaps. Then the sitter should reach up to try to touch the stander. How does your arm feel after about 30 seconds? Is the picture of the stander distorted in any way from the eye-level view? How?

Switch positions and discuss your perceptions and feelings. This exercise should help to remind you to try to maintain eye-level contact with your children whenever you can, to avoid appearing like a "giant" to them.

"Who's assertive?"—a checklist

Use the following checklist to discover how assertive you can allow your children to be, and how assertive you are with them. Each item requires only a "yes" or "no" answer.

_____ Do I demand from my children only what they can realistically complete at one time?

_____ When I make requests of my children, do I provide follow-through help?

_____ In most situations does my child understand what I expect from her/him? Are my requests specific as to time, place, etc.?

_____ When I make requests or demands of my children, do I also specify how the demands can be met?

_____ Do I provide my child with some privacy, or do I feel threatened when I am not in direct control (talking on the telephone without my knowing to whom she/he is talking)?

_____ Do I treat my child as though she/he has personal rights (privacy in her/his own room)?

_____ Do I set realistic limits for my child (curfew, TV time, household chores)?

_____ Do I encourage my child to handle some situations independently but with my support (helping with my child's homework, letting my child resolve difficulties with friends)?

_____ Do I allow my child openly to disagree with my judgment (allowing my child to choose her/his own friends)?

_____ Do I encourage my child to stand up for her/his rights with others as well as with me?

_____ When unable to control my child, do I resort to threats, shouting, or striking the child?

_____ Do I listen to my child's point of view?

_____ Does my view always prevail or do I also let my child "win" sometimes?

_____ Do I refrain from over-protecting my child (not wanting my child to be involved in any sports activities for fear of injury)?

_____ Do I allow my child to state how she/he feels without *telling* her/him how she/he feels?

After you have completed the above checklist, consider your responses carefully. Your answers may reflect particular areas that could be handled more assertively.

The rights of small people

The assertive woman recognizes that her children are also people, with rights of their own. She encourages her children to act independently, but also provides specific guidelines for them. When the assertive woman makes a demand or request of her child, she specifies clearly what she expects, and how her child can meet her expectations. In return for the child's respect toward the home in which she/he lives, the assertive woman also respects the child's territory. By assertive communication and behavior the assertive woman avoids the Aggression and Slavery Traps and avoids passing on the Compassion Trap.

If you apply the principles and suggestions offered in this chapter to your interactions with your children, you will be less likely to terrorize or be terrorized by your children. If your home has been a constant battlefield, you can look forward to improved communication and possibly increased peace. There is no simple, fool-proof formula for living with children, or for living with anyone else, but the assertive woman is headed in the right direction.

XIII. Women Together

*"If we hope to do anything for ourselves as
individuals, we must join with all other
women. When we begin to appreciate each
other for what we are and can be, avoiding
negative comparisons, we will begin to build
the grassroots movement that will change
what it means to be female."*
—*Aleen Holly and Anne Rogers*
"On Feeling Superior to Other Women"
Conscious-Raising Group, 1971.

Becoming an assertive woman involves reaching out and interacting with other people on many levels. In our exercises we have
suggested that you initially try out new assertive ways of saying and
doing things with people who are potentially supportive and understanding of your goals. So often the understanding and support will
come from another woman who is, or has been, experiencing the
same feeling. Our assertiveness must begin with each other.

We need to turn our compassion appropriately toward one
another. This is a natural way for women as a whole to be able to
develop strong assertive patterns. Many women who have turned to
husbands, boyfriends, or family for support in becoming assertive
have been met with resistance and/or fear, even though they have
usually received support from these intimates for other things.

Your becoming assertive is *different*. It has the potential to
change close relationships and the whole status quo of your family.

For this reason it can be very threatening both to you and to them. It is unfair and unwise to expect most of your support to come from someone whose world you may be turning upside down.

We are not suggesting that you should not expect to obtain support from the intimate people in your life. On the contrary, it will be vital to keep communication open to let each other know how you are feeling and what is happening. However, it may help for you to encourage your intimates to seek support from others at times and *not* from you. It would be ever so easy for you to fall into the Compassion Trap with them and stop your efforts toward becoming assertive. Of course, they may experience some discomfort, inconvenience, and pain in the short run. But, you must remind yourself and them that the ultimate effects of your becoming an assertive woman will make all of you happier and freer people.

Throughout the book we have made references to different methods that may enhance your ability to become an assertive woman. First of all—you need to be open to and ask for *honest feedback* from your supporters.

For example, Doris asks her friend, April, who has accompanied her to the department store to return an article of clothing: "In what ways do you think I handled returning that blouse assertively, and where could I use some practice?" April honestly replies, "You really made good eye contact with him, your voice was clear and strong, and you did not back down from your original request. However, your body seemed too rigid and tense, and your facial expression was nervous and almost too stern. You can still appear firm without looking so tight and intense."

Once the feedback process is underway, it is important to set yourself up to be *rewarded* or *reinforced* for your assertive efforts. You can negotiate with your friends and/or women's group to praise and encourage you whenever you have tried to do something assertive, even if you have failed. It is important to feel good about the effort you put into each step and about any small improvements you may have made.

Get into the habit of making positive comments to others when you see them being assertive. You will be rewarded by their reciprocating when you need to be noticed for your efforts. Whatever you do, be honest, and encourage others to be honest with you.

Sometimes it is tempting to collude with another person and avoid giving negative feedback and only say what you know they want to hear. But while this approach often wins instantaneous popularity, you are certain to lose credibility when the person finds out you were not being straightforward.

Another method you can use to become more assertive is *role-playing* and/or *script writing.* Sharon Bower uses this method frequently. If you are uptight about an impending situation in which you will want to be assertive, you can write out a script of how you would like the situation to go. Then check your script out with a friend, or role-play the script to see how it actually sounds and feels.

On the other hand, you may want to skip the script and just try to work out your situation by spontaneously role-playing or play-acting with a friend. You might have your friend play your part so you can see how you look or would like to look. Sometimes it is easier for you to switch roles and to play the part of the person with whom you want to be assertive, because it is often easier to anticipate her/his moves than to portray your own.

In trying to avoid putting yourself down or being non-assertive, there is a chance that you may overreact by thinking of yourself as "really assertive" to the extent that you do not feel it necessary to ask for help or support from other women. In fact, there may be a temptation to see yourself as different, or on a higher level and much more assertive than other women. Your independence may be a symptom of the Queen Bee syndrome.

The "Queen Bee" syndrome

The temptation to distinguish yourself apart from other women by seeing yourself as more assertive, as functioning on a higher level, and as being more sophisticated, is to risk falling into the "Queen Bee Syndrome." Staines, Tavris, and Jayaratne discuss this syndrome in "The Queen Bee Syndrome," *Psychology Today*, January 1974. The Queen Bee feels superior to other women, to the point of identifying with men. She enjoys hearing that she is certainly different from most women.

If you allow yourself to fall into the Queen Bee syndrome, you will risk becoming as insensitive as Agatha. In being assertive, like April, you remain aware of the rights of others to be assertive too.

You allow others to choose for themselves; you are creating a supportive, caring atmosphere where you and others can grow and change.

"Where do I go from here?"

At this point you may be asking yourself, "Where do I go from here?" If reading this book is your first introduction to the idea of becoming more assertive as a woman, you may be feeling very much alone right now. You may be doubting your actual desire or need to become more assertive. If this is the case, before you decide whether or not to embark upon the journey of assertiveness, find out how other women feel. There are many ways to do this.

"How do I talk to other women?"

There are many examples which could be taken from our workshop experiences. You might begin by referring to an article or book you have been reading:

"I just read *The Assertive Woman*, and I wonder if you know about it. Do you?"

Or you could find out about the other woman's feelings about assertion:

"How do you feel about being assertive?"

"In what ways do you think you are being a more assertive woman?"

Or you could ask the other woman to report on her observations of you:

"I would really like to be a more assertive person, but I am overwhelmed about where to begin. Do you have any suggestions for me?"

Some resources

First of all, you can have another woman read this book and you can discuss its pros and cons. Or, you may have the opportunity to take an extension class or a workshop on assertive training for women through a college or evening school program. Another resource is the programs which more and more community mental health centers are beginning to offer for women in seach of assertive skills. Some private therapists offer individual or group assertive training. Many of these groups are mixed; you may find an all-female assertive group more relevant and helpful to you than a mixed group.

If you are unable to be involved in a workshop or therapy program, you can still structure your own systematic self-help program. We recommend use of this book in conjunction with *Your Perfect Right*, and other materials we have mentioned. You may also wish to subscribe to *Assert: The Newsletter of Assertive Behavior*, a publication reporting on assertive training resources across the country. (*Bibliography*).

If you live in or near a city, there is a strong possibility that you will have the free services of a Women's Center or a Women's Health Clinic available to you. These are excellent resources. The National Organization for Women (NOW) can help you locate women's assertive groups, and consciousness raising groups, too. If you take your children to a Day Care Center, you may find a receptive group of women ready to learn assertion with you.

Community colleges across the country are beginning "re-entry programs" for women who have been out of school or in a career for a long time and now want to begin anew. College counselors are interested in having women's rap (discussion) groups and/or assertive groups. Perhaps you can help to get one going on a campus near you.

Another resource is in women's self-defense classes, many of which are being re-structured to integrate assertive methods. You can contact your local recreation department or your community college to find out when self-defense classes for women are being offered.

Even in the business world, in which women have played such a basic role, there are now management training groups for women which include training in assertive skills. If you do not have such a management group available to you now, begin a discussion about it at your women's group meeting, or on the job. There may be funds available to hire a professional consultant to conduct an assertive training workshop with your group or your staff.

Creating your own women's group

No matter what your life style or where you live, you should be able to find your own unique support group or vehicle for becoming an assertive woman. If, after looking around, you are unable to find an already existing group, you can begin a group of your own. In the March, 1973 issue of *Ms.* (pp. 80-81), Letty Cottin Pogrebin has written a very sensitive and informative article on "Rap Groups" that goes into very specific detail about how to begin a woman's consciousness-raising group. Speaking from her own personal experience she says: ". . . I wanted not to stand apart from other women, but to bond with them. Women's groups have facilitated that bonding. Better still, I have found that I need and can accept the help and support of other women. But best of all, I've discovered that consciousness-raising groups are far from my original image of passive, complaining women. The truth is that, along with their function as a release valve for rage and frustration, C-R groups are exhilarating, challenging, life-enhancing, and, very often, great fun."

How to start your own Women's C-R Group

We have participated in many such groups and helped to initiate several. Here are some steps you can follow:

How to Start Your Own Consciousness-Raising Group

- Begin by talking enthusiastically to women of all ages about the need for a C-R group in your locale.

- When you have stimulated the interest of from 6 to 10 women, invite them to your house for an introductory C-R evening (perhaps two hours).

- Take responsibility for the first evening's topic—and make it a basic topic that is non-threatening and one with which all women can relate from their own personal experiences, e.g. "Who is or has been the most significant woman in your life? How was she significant?

- Each woman should be encouraged to talk for about 5 minutes, but she may pass if she feels uncomfortable. It is easiest to sit in a circle and start with one woman (preferably yourself as a model), until each woman around the circle has taken her turn.

- After each woman has had a turn, you may lead a discussion on how you as women have certain things in common, pin-pointing common themes and patterns of thought and behavior. Summarize the group's conclusions.

- After this discussion, ask for feedback from all women on how they enjoyed the C-R process, being sure to again speak of your enthusiasm and support for it.

- Suggest that the group make a commitment to meet for a certain number of weeks or months. Agree that new members may join until the third session.

- Set up some ground rules such as:
  1. Agree to meet two hours once a week.
  2. Seek to begin and end groups on time.
  3. Promise to respect each other's vulnerability and therefore agree to keep all information confidential.
  4. Insist that the group be emotionally supportive of each other and avoid the temptation to criticize, judge or confront each other. Remember this is not a encounter group. Your goal is to raise each other's awareness level in a non-threatening manner
  5. Decide either on a regular meeting place or to rotate meeting locations.
  6. Plan to keep eating and drinking at a minimum and to share these expenses.
  7. Do not charge a membership fee.
  8. If possible, rotate leadership from week to week.
  9. The leader will help the group to decide upon a topic for the following week so that each woman has ample time to think about it and get in touch with her feelings before the next meeting.
  10. Do not try to undertake therapy with anyone. If therapy seems indicated, encourage the individual to seek professional therapy.

• Write for information and suggested topics for C-R groups from women's centers as well as the nearest NOW Center (National Organization for Women).

• Suggest that topics be developed progressively from general, basic and non-threatening issues to the more specific, threatening and/or complex issues

Creating a men's C-R group

Perhaps you have a male friend who is interested in exploring how to begin a group for men. Or, perhaps you are a man, who happens to be reading this book. We realized we were writing *The Assertive Woman* that many of the concepts and exercises that we have introduced for women can be equally appropriate for men.

For this reason we want to refer you to another article by Warren Farrell, "Men: Guidelines for Consciousness-Raising," *Ms.*, February, 1973. He says:

"A Men's Liberation Movement is evolving, and it's looking at Women's Liberation and men's roles in a new way. We have learned a lot from the Women's Movement (and it wasn't easy for most of us to learn from women). We have seen, for example, the roots of our underlying contempt for women as we've systematically exposed the devastating feminine stereotypes—stereotypes to which many of us reacted by a determination to prove ourselves masculine. We found, though, that the roles had to be changed in a wider ranging way than the Women's Movement was then exploring: rather than picturing women in children's books, for instance, as doctors or astronauts, it was important also to have men pictured as caring for children, as elementary teachers, admitting they were wrong, or asking women a question, wearing an apron in the kitchen, or ironing a women's pants suit, or even crying."

In his article, Farrell proceed to discuss the men who go to C-R groups, when and where they meet, and the problems they encounter, as well as suggestions on how to handle such problems. He includes a very useful list of topics for discussion. We highly recommend his article as a beginning resource.

If you are interested in starting a men's C-R group, you may find the following guidelines helpful:

- Talk with other men about whether a C-R group would be beneficial for them.

- Get a small group of six to ten men interested and invite them to a meeting at a home.

- Find out at the meeting what type of commitment each man is willing to make in terms of attending regular meetings, and for how long meetings should run.

- Establish basic ground rules for discussion.

- Try to set up a regular day and time to meet and agree upon a meeting place or places.

- Select a topic of discussion a week in advance; think about it before the meeting, and stick to it when you talk.

- Try to keep the same group of men together long enough (weeks or months) to get to know each other and explore issues in depth.

- Concentrate on men's C-R and on problems of your relationships with other men and with women. Talk about the ways in which "masculinity" may hinder your own liberation.

Step-by-Step together

In this chapter we have tried to emphasize the importance of women seeking each other out, of being together, talking, sharing, and caring for each other. Being an assertive woman can be a more realistic and attainable goal if you have the support of other women throughout your struggles and triumphs.

In our workshops we have found that initially women are more apt to try new assertive behaviors if there are no men present. Therefore, in the beginning we prefer to have all-female groups because it seems to reduce inhibitions and expedite a woman's growth.

Having the support and encouragement of other women can accelerate your progress toward becoming an assertive woman. Your particular circumstances may limit the support you can receive from others. Although you may find yourself without emotional support from others, apply yourself to following the guidelines in this book and you will begin to acquire valuable assertive skills. We further urge you to seek out support from others so that your assertiveness can develop into a new life style for you.

As a woman gains confidence and becomes more like April, she is ready to participate in mixed groups if she chooses to do so. At first, however, it is necessary for a woman to discover that other women count, that their support and approval can make her day, as well as help her to achieve a more assertive life style. Many times we have observed in our workshops that a woman who joins a mixed group (women and men) too soon, will carry on with old habit patterns, e.g. looking to the men in the group for support and approval and overlooking the other women as sources of support.

Our conditioning has been so pervasive that we must take every opportunity we can to structure our experiences in ways that facilitate new learning and change. We as women must focus on the problems of women instead of allowing ourselves to be seduced into our traditional roles of being nurturing and supportive to men and oriented toward men's problems. We need to form our own opinions and standards; we cannot assume that male standards are better for us, or, in fact, that they are good for men either. By continually deferring to male opinion and methods, we do a disservice to both sexes.

Perhaps as men grow through their own consciousness-raising, they will abandon archaic male standards, also. It is possible that women and men will reach for new and mutually shared non-sexist goals.

We like men. Our purpose is to make the transition easier for women to be assertive and enjoy their relationships both with men and with other women. We do not want to exclude men from women's lives. Instead, we wish to prepare women to relate to people with less anxiety and with greater skills in communication.

Our answer to the question, "Can I make it alone?" is a qualified, "Yes."

Often in our workshops we see examples of how women benefit from mutual support. The separated or divorced woman who is struggling to assert herself with her ex-husband is typical. For many reasons, mostly economic or child-related, the divorced woman feels very much in a double-bind with her ex, to whom she is still tied in some way(s).

She frequently is afraid to assert herself because she believes that it will anger her ex, who will then punish her by hurting the children, cutting off his financial support, or by embarrassing or otherwise harrassing her. In order to avoid retaliation, she complies passively with most of his requests or demands. In doing so many women fail to exercise their rights to human dignity and a new life.

Do you recognize yourself or someone you know in the following example?

Will you still do my laundry?

Hubert: "Now listen, Doris, I'm giving you and the kids as much money as I can. And, believe me, it's a real hardship on me. I work hard for my money. Look at you! What do you do for me? Nothing . . . You're so selfish. All you ever think about is yourself. You have the house. And to think that you complained about my parents staying here for two weeks vacation. Did you expect me to put them in a motel after all they've done for you? Now you're complaining because I'm asking you to do my laundry and run a few simple errands."

Doris: (feeling guilty and threatened that he will stop paying child support) "You're right. I do appreciate all that you're doing for us. It's just that with the kids, and my real estate class, and my part-time job, I don't seem to have any time left for myself. But, (feeling resentful) I can understand how difficult things are for you and I'll try not to complain about your laundry anymore."

When a woman shares examples of her non-assertiveness in such situations, other women from the group who have been in similar positions can relate to her struggle. They are able to empathize totally and to give suggestions as to how to handle an ex-husband who still sees his wife as an indispensible servant.

For example, the women reminded Doris of her rights as an independent person—an individual with the right to privacy, to legal support, to relaxation, and to choose how much contact she will attempt to have with her ex-spouse. The women encouraged Doris to assertively say "no" without falling into the Compassion Trap; they exchanged phone numbers with Doris and made plans to help her to begin a social life of her own.

Women together can benefit by:

- Reminding each other of their basic human rights.

- Giving each other emotional support and feedback.

- Being able to relate to and understand each other due to similar experiences.

- Providing suggestions for change.

- Being available for each other in times of stress.

- Giving approval and positive reinforcement for each other's new attempts toward assertion.

- Sharing joy in each other's triumphs over past hang-ups and non-assertions.

XIV. Freedom

"The worst thing one can do is not to try, to be aware of what one wants and not give in to it, to spend years in silent hurt wondering if something could have materialized—and never knowing."
—David S. Viscott,
Feel Free

We hope that this book helps you to explore new, direct alternatives open to you, and that it encourages you to respect your feelings as well as the feelings of others. As an assertive woman, you promote your own personal freedom.

Assertion is an on-going process. The best way to protect your rights is to continue to use them. There are direct benefits for you and for others. Others can learn from you to be more assertive people, and you can give each other a great deal of support. As you assert yourself you will feel strength and a sense of personal worth. The important thing to remember is to continue to act assertively. View your assertiveness and personal freedom as something you do each day for yourself.

Most women in our workshops tell us that they realize the potential benefits involved in becoming assertive women. They are usually motivated to change their behavior, particularly if they have experienced success with initial attempts at assertion. Yet they are concerned with the possible negative or painful consequences they fear assertion may produce: "What if my whole family life is disrupted—my husband leaves me—my parents kick me out of the house—my employer fires me? Is it worth that?"

We believe that you may experience some initial discomfort as you begin to assert yourself, particularly if those around you fear that they stand to lose something. We also feel that a major life disruption—divorce or separation—is possible if your family and those close to you are not sufficiently prepared for your assertive behavior. They may be more threatened than pleased. In such circumstances, the help of professional counseling or a program of assertive training for your family is a good idea.

Even in less extreme situations, you may find that you have to go through some temporarily negative consequences to enjoy the long term benefits of being an assertive woman. The specific situations will, of course, differ, but the negative consequences usually involve the emotional turbulence that accompanies any major change in our lives. If you resist acting assertively because you fear negative consequences, remember the price you have already been paying for your non-assertiveness. You may have been taken advantage of by others, or manipulated by others for their own gain. Or you may be driving away those whom you most desire to be near. You probably feel hurt, anxious, helpless, put upon, guilty or ignored in the process.

We have found that there are many more long-term benefits and positive consequences involved when you act assertively. Consider the positive benefits that prompted you to seek a change: a sense of well-being, self-respect, and control over your life. Realizing that the consequences of not acting are worse than the consequences of acting will give you the support you need to assert yourself at first. Some of the women in our workshops feel that they have tolerated chronic pain for most of their lives. They may still find it difficult to believe in the benefits of action. They have been taught that it is somehow part of woman's nature to be able to endure pain. Being a woman has meant knowing how to suffer.

As Harry Browne emphasizes in *How I Found Freedom in an Unfree World*, don't be so afraid of sudden, temporary discomfort that you willingly tolerate continued, deadening pain for the rest of your life. If you resist being assertive because you fear possible, temporary negative consequences, you are really resigning yourself to living with chronic pain and little happiness in your life. You don't have to consent to living your life out in continual pain and discomfort. You have the freedom to choose to assert yourself and to receive love, respect, and admiration for being an assertive woman.

You will find that situations will arise in which you may choose not to assert yourself, even though you could. Alberti and Emmons discuss several of these situations, involving overly-sensitive individuals or special circumstances, for example, when someone you know is having an 'off' day, you may *choose* to postpone a confrontation to a more productive time.

If you find that someone close to you is having "bad days" more and more frequently, you may be a victim of manipulation. While you may occasionally choose not to assert yourself out of consideration of another's feelings, you should remember the Compassion Trap. Someone close to you may be using it to try to get you to be less assertive. Talking about the situation with the people involved might help to alleviate their anxiety.

Asserting yourself in your personal life carries with it positive, constructive rewards for you as a person. The assertive woman can also work to change things on a larger scale. Here are a few suggestions:

Education

Traditional educational systems encourage passive acceptance of the rules. Students are lectured to, made to adhere to impersonal schedules, required to listen rather than discuss, and urged to work for grades and averages. In this system, students have very limited power. They may even hesitate to ask questions because they fear being reprimanded or ridiculed by the instructor for asking such a "stupid" question. The teachers ask the questions and the students provide the answers. Assertive students who challenge conventional practices are labeled "troublemakers."

Fortunately, this system is giving way under the influence of many assertive individuals who believe that silent obedience and compliance are not a valuable part of education. Alternatives to the traditional educational model are being explored and adopted by a wide cross-section of people. Students are being given a chance to do more than passively complete homework assignments.

Educational systems, although changing, have a distance to go before they will be more supportive of the individual. Assertive students, teachers, community officials, and parents can direct their energies toward improving the educational system. Assertive individuals *can* make a difference.

Government

Assertive women have worked to change governmental policies and legislation quite effectively. Under the strongly felt influence of the National Organization of Women (NOW), rape laws are being changed to eliminate sexism.

Increasing numbers of women are running for and being elected to legislative positions. Within local as well as national government, asserting yourself can produce effective results. Governmental programs and policies have been slow in changing, and there is still room for improvement. You can be effective if you assert yourself persistently, but you should realize that government moves slowly and you will need patience if you choose this area to begin your assertiveness. Find others to work with and provide reinforcement.

Business

Large organizations in the business world have been famous for their conservative, sexist practices. Airlines, employing large numbers of women as stewardesses, have changed their policies under the influence of the women themselves. Most airlines now refer to their stewardesses and stewards as "flight attendants." Women employed as flight attendants asserted themselves to change sexist hiring practices; airlines now hire women regardless of their marital status.

Women are entering the business world professionally, also. Still, women are usually asked "Can you type?" Their career options are still limited in the business world, but the pressure is being felt.

Housewifery

The institution of housewifery has undergone important changes. Concepts such as equal pay for equal work helped distinguish housewifery as a full-time occupation. Women are feeling free to define themselves less as housewives and more as individual people with varied interests. Women have asserted themselves to break away from the idea that "the woman's place is in the home."

They are no longer "just housewives." The term "househusband" is now being used as housekeeping is defined less in terms of an exclusively feminine pursuit.

Being an Agent for Change

These examples certainly don't include all of the possibilities for effective assertion on a large scale. The list below suggests some additional areas in which you, as an assertive woman, can be an agent for change:

Education: You can obtain non-sexist readers for your children, as well as urging changes in the type of texts used in your child's school. You can organize support for classes for boys in marriage, family, and child rearing; and seek more opportunities for girls in sports activities and industrial arts and automotive classes. On the college level you can advocate non-sexist admissions requirements.

Child-rearing: It's time to stop leaving the men out! Let's push for mutuality of parenting. Give men the chance to enjoy their children more and give women as much free time as their spouses.

Government: Get involved in politics on a local level by actively supporting a candidate for office who is sensitive to women's issues. Or, better yet, get elected yourself!

Military: Talk to recruitment officers about opportunities for advancement and more creative opportunities for women. Object to military sexist discrimination whenever you see examples.

Housewifery: In this day of fancy job titles feel free to list yourself as a "domestic engineer" if you choose to spend the greater part of your time administering a household. Also, you may want to negotiate for a salary and paid vacation.

Hiring Practices: If your local newspaper has not done so already, write a letter to the editor requesting that the classified ads do not segregate women from men in listing employment opportunities. Suggest to employment agencies, personnel departments and educational facilities that they expand options open to women to include careers such as firefighting, auto mechanics, accounting, dentistry and piloting commercial aircraft. Conversely, suggest that men be encouraged to become elementary school teachers, dieticians, receptionists and secretaries.

Dress Regulations: Work to abolish unfair dress regulations for either men or women in public places such as restaurants and churches, as well as on the job.

Business Practices: Be more assertive and ask for raises, promotions, and appropriate job titles when they are due. Don't look down on women who do not have a job as good as yours. Resist the urge to seek prior approval from male supervisors or colleagues when you have the authority to make a decision on your own. Business is one area where you cannot afford to sit back and wait for someone else to acknowledge your achievements.

Legal Restrictions: Join forces with other women who are working toward eliminating legalized sexist discrimination with regard to rape, abortion, day care legislation, divorce, and maternity benefits. Object to discriminating insurance policy clauses, sick leave restrictions (extended time and maternity benefits for women and men), requirements for spouses as co-signers on loan or credit card applications.

Consumer Affairs: Establish your own sources of credit and refuse to be categorized only as Mrs. or Miss_____. Don't let yourself or other women be used and manipulated as pawns of economic forces that exploit women as super-consumers.

Medical Practices: Find out the facts about what may be unnecessary surgery for you or other women, for example, hysterectomies and radical mastectomies. Be cautious of doctors who frequently prescribe tranquilizers for women because of their "psychosomatic and/or hysterical" symptoms.

Media: Call radio and TV stations to comment on non-sexist programming that you liked or on sexist programming or advertising that you dislike. Support women in broadcasting by listening to them and telling their sponsors that you enjoy listening to them. And don't forget to compliment men for non-sexist broadcasting.

Athletics: Urge equal funding and participation for high school and collegiate women's athletic programs. Voice your opinion about opening more professional sports to women, as well as equalizing prize money for women's and men's professional athletic events.

Not all assertions are personal and verbal in nature. When you are dealing with organizations or institutions, a personal contact may not be immediately possible or desirable. The assertive woman can still be assertive and initiate changes using other methods. For example:

1. Writing letters or sending telegrams to government officials, presidents of corporations, or educational boards.

2. Forming local activist groups (Common Cause).

3. Attending rallies and meetings, being "where the action is" (school board).

4. Making your achievements visible by writing articles, or making speeches. Also setting up a system of "honors and credits" to acknowledge women's contributions.

5. Increasing participation in existing activist groups.

6. Breaking into traditionally-male fields (government, business executive positions).

7. Working on political campaigns.

8. Getting on city, church, or political committees.

9. Rejecting the "feminine mystique" perpetuated by consumerism, the media, and other institutions.

You can be free—free from guilt, anxiety, fear, and constraints that you never thought you could control or change. Being free also means choosing to be assertive when you want to be assertive. You may choose not to assert yourself for many reasons ranging from sensitivity to others's feelings at a particularly difficult time to feeling that a given situation calls for a passive or an aggressive response. For example, you may not want to assert yourself with a belligerent person or a person undergoing severe stress.

It is also important not to see assertion as a cure-all for all problems or as a simplistic way to achieve personal strength and a sense of self-worth. For example, people struggling with very real economic and social problems such as inadequate housing, providing food for themselves and their families, dealing with probation, carrying out a prison term or adjusting to life in a new and unfamiliar culture, may find that individual assertion is not enough. This is perhaps an opportunity for collective assertion. Remember that assertiveness is not an end in itself. Also work out other ways to achieve dignity and happiness in your life.

Assertion is much more than a strategy for self-defense. The assertive woman can use her assertive skills to reach out in a warm, humorous, expressive way, as a very positive, human communication. There is no "standard" or single correct way to be an assertive woman. We have seen many women develop an assertive style that works for them, bringing to it their own personal touch, and we support this individualism for each reader.

We have intended this book for you, the individual woman. Nevertheless, we have necessarily written from our individual perspectives and biases. Because we could only talk about experiences known to us, we may not have included experiences directly relevant to you. For this reason we have included the Feedback section which follows.

Finally, the thought we would like to leave with you is that becoming an assertive woman is a giant step toward personal freedom and growth. We urge you to take this first step and let us hear from you. Good luck, patience, perserverance, assertiveness—and love.

XV. Feedback

"If I am not for myself, who will be for me?
If I am not for others, who am I for? And if
not now, when?"
—The Talmud

This book is more than a book to us, it is a process. And you are a very important part of that process. We would like you to complete a final exercise. Your comments and feelings about *The Assertive Woman* are important to us and we welcome your correspondence. Your answers to the following questions will provide us with feedback about your personal experiences with assertion, and help us to make this book continually more helpful to others. Just complete the questionnaire and send it to us, signed or unsigned. Write us a letter relating your adventures in becoming an assertive person. Tell us what you would like us to pass on to others.

1. *The Assertive Woman* helped me to behave more assertively with:
   (check as many as apply)
   _____ family members
   _____ close friends
   _____ employers, employees
   _____ spouse, mate, lover
   _____ other women
   _____ other men
   _____ others:_____

2. After reading *The Assertive Woman*, I find it easier to feel assertive and behave assertively when:

____ I am being criticized
____ I am criticizing someone else
____ I am the center of attention
____ I am arguing
____ I am angry
____ I am expressing love and affection
____ I ask for love and attention
____ I talk with authority figures
____ Other:_____

3. Below is a list of major topics appearing in *The Assertive Woman*. Please mark an "x" beside the areas that had the most meaning or importance for you, and a check (✔) beside the items that you found least important. Mark items with a zero (0) if all areas were equally important.

____ your body—developing assertive behaviors
____ your mind—developing an assertive attitude
____ from apology to power
____ sensuality
____ children
____ manipulation and counter-manipulation
____ saying "no"
____ anger
____ humor
____ compliments, criticism and rejection
____ women together
____ freedom

4. What additional topics and information would like to see included in this book?

____ more about adolescents
____ more about political, social, economic concerns
____ more about job/careers
____ others:_____

5. With whom have you shared this book?

____ other women
____ spouse, mate, or lover

____ parents
____ children
____ relatives, close friends
____ women's groups or organizations
____ men's groups or organizations
____ my students; classmates
____ others:_____

6. What section of this book did you particularly like? _____
_____

Dislike? _____
_____

7. Optional information about yourself: (answer any or all)
____Female   Marital status: Single____ Married____ Divorced____
____Male   Widowed____
____Under 18   ____18 to 26   ____26 to 40   ____over 40
Occupation _____Level or Education_____
Name _____
Address _____City_____State_____Zip_____

Other books I have read concerning self development.

____ I would like to receive a sample copy of ASSERT: THE
   NEWSLETTER FOR ASSERTIVE BEHAVIOR. I am interested
   in information about assertiveness training as follows:
____ conference & workshop schedules
____ assertion for children
____ assertion in business & industry
____ publications
____ assertion & minorities
____ research & tests
____ other (specify): _____

Bibliography

Adams, Elsie, and Briscoe, Marie L.   *Up Against the Wall, Mother.* Beverly Hills: Glencoe Press, 1971.

Adams, Margaret.   "The Compassion Trap," *Women in Sexist Society: Studies in Power and Powerlessness.* Edited by B. Moran and V. Gornick.

Alberti, Robert E., and Emmons, Michael L.   *Your Perfect Right.* San Luis Obispo: Impact, 1970, 1974.

Atlantic.   "Women's Place," March, 1970, pp. 81-126.

Bach, George R., and Wyden, Peter.   *The Intimate Enemy.* New York: William Morrow Co., 1969.

Becker, W.C.   *Parents Are Teachers: A Child Management Program.* Champaign, Illinois: Research Press, 1971.

Berne, Eric.   *Games People Play.* New York: Grove Press, 1964.

Bird, Caroline.   *Born Female: The High Cost of Keeping Women Down.* New York: David McKay Co., 1968.

Boston Women's Health Book Collective.   *Our Bodies, Ourselves.* New York: Simon and Schuster, 1973.

Bower, Sharon Anthony.   *Learning Assertive Behavior With PALS.* Unpublished paper, Foothill College, Los Altos, California, 1972.

Brecher, Ruth and Breecher, Edward, (eds.).   *An Analysis of Human Sexual Response.* New York: New American Library, 1973.

Browne, Harry.   *How I Found Freedom in an Unfree World.* New York: Avon Books, 1972.

Butler, Pamela E.   "Techniques of Assertive Training in Groups." Unpublished paper, The Behavior Institute, Sausalito, California.

Burton, Gabrielle.   *I'm Running Away from Home but I'm Not Allowed to Cross the Street.* Pittsburgh: Know, Inc., 1972.

Chesler, Phyllis.   *Women and Madness.* New York: Avon Books, 1972.

Chisholm, Shirley. *Unbought and Unbossed.* Boston: Houghton Mifflin Co., 1970.

DeCrow, Karen. *The Young Woman's Guide to Liberation.* Indianapolis: Pegasus Books, 1971.

Dodsen, Betty. *Liberating Masturbation: A Meditation on Self-Love.* New York: Bodysex Designs, 1974.

Eisler, R.M., Miller, P.M., and Hersen, M. "Components of Assertive Behavior," *Journal of Clinical Psychology*, Vol. 29, No. 3, (1973) pp. 295-299.

Ellis, A., and Harper, R. *A Guide to Rational Living.* Englewood Cliffs, N.J.: Prentice-Hall, 1961.

Ellis, Albert. *How to Prevent your Child from Becoming a Neurotic Adult.* New York: Crown Press, 1966.

Ellis, Albert. *The Sensuous Person: Critique and Corrections.* Secaucus, New Jersey: Lyle Stuart Inc., 1972.

Esterson, A., and Laing, R.D. *Sanity, Madness and the Family.* New York: Basic Books, 1964.

Farrell, Warren. "Men: Guidelines for Consciousness-Raising," *Ms.*, February, 1973.

Fast, Julius. *Body Language.* Philadelphia: M. Evans Co., 1970.

Friedan, Betty. *The Feminine Mystique.* New York: W.W. Norton and Co., 1963.

Garskof, Michele Hoffnung (ed.). *Roles Women Play: Readings Toward Women's Liberation.* Belmont, California: Brooks/Cole Publishing Co., 1971.

Ginott, Haim G. *Between Parent & Child.* New York: Macmillan, 1965.

Gornick, Vivian, and Moran, Barbara (eds.). *Women in Sexist Society: Studies in Power and Powerlessness.* New York: Basic Books, 1971.

Greer, Germaine. *The Female Eunuch.* New York: McGraw-Hill, 1970.

Harris. T. *I'm OK; You're OK: A Practical Guide to Transactional Analysis.* New York: Harper & Row, 1967.

Hersen, M., Eisler, R.M., and Miller, P.M. "Development of Assertive Responses: Clinical, Measurement, and Research Considerations," *Behaviour Research and Therapy*, (1973) Vol. 11, pp. 505-521.

Jacobsen, E. *Progressive Relaxation.* Chicago: University of Chicago Press, 1938.

Lazarus, Arnold A. (ed.) *Clinical Behavior Therapy.* New York: Bruner/Mazel, Inc., 1972.

Lessing, Doris. *The Golden Notebook*. New York: Ballantine Books, 1962.

Lorenz, Konrad. *On Agression*. New York: Harcourt, Brace and World, 1966.

Madow, Leo. *Anger*. New York: Scribner's Sons, 1972.

Marine, Gene. *A Male Guide to Women's Liberation*. New York: Avon Books, 1972.

Montague, Ashley. *The Natural Superiority of Women*. New York: Collier Books, 1970 (revised).

Morgan, Robin (ed.). *Sisterhood is Powerful*. New York: Random House, 1970.

O'Neill, Nena and George. *Open Marriage*. New York: M. Evans and Co., 1972.

Patterson, G.R. *Families/Application of Social Learning to Family Life*. Champaign: Research Press, 1971.

Patterson, G.R. and Gullion, M.E. *Living with Children: New Methods for Parents and Teachers*. Champaign, Illinois: Research Press, 1968.

Pogrebin, Letty Cottin. "Rap Groups: The Feminist Connection," *Ms.*, March, 1973, pp. 80-104.

Ruesch, J., and Kees, W. *Non-Verbal Communication*. Berkeley and Los Angeles: University of California Press, 1956.

Rush, Anne Kent. *Getting Clear: Body Work for Women*. New York: Random House, 1973.

Satir, Virginia. *Peoplemaking*. Palo Alto: Science and Behavior Books, 1972.

Schutz, William. *Joy*. New York: Grove Press, 1967.

Seaman, Barbara. *Free and Female: The Sex Life of the Contemporary Woman*. New York: Coward McCann and Geohegan, 1972.

Shastrom, Everett. *Man the Manipulator*. New York: Abingdon Press, 1967.

Staines, G., Tavris, C., and Jayaratne, T.E. "The Queen Bee Syndrome," *Psychology Today*, January, 1974, pp. 55-60.

Tanner, Leslie B. (ed.). *Voices from Women's Liberation*. New York: New American Library, 1970.

Turner, A. Jack. Deep Muscle Relaxation Induction Procedure. *Cybersystems, Inc.*, P.O. Box 3365, M.S. A.B., Huntsville, Alabama 35810.

Viscott, David S. *Feel Free*. New York: Wyden Press, 1971.

Wolpe, Joseph. *The Practice of Behavior Therapy*. New York: Pergamon Press, 1973.

Wolpe, J., and Lazarus, A.A. *Behavior Therapy Techniques.* New York· Pergamon Press, 1966.

Woolf, Virginia. *A Room of One's Own.* New York: Harcourt, Brace and World (originally published 1929).

Zunin, Leonard, and Zunin, Natalie. *Contact: The First Four Minutes.* New York: Ballantine Books, Inc., 1972.

Permission to reprint or quote portions of the following is also gratefully acknowledged:

The Intimate Enemy, by George R. Bach and Peter Wyden. Copyright, 1969, by William Morrow Company. Used by permission of the authors.

Learning Assertive Behavior with PALS, by Sharon A. Bower. Copyright, 1974. Used by permission of the author.

How I Found Freedom in an Unfree World, by Harry Browne. Copyright, 1972, by Avon Books. Used by permission of the author.

Consciousness Raising Handbook, by the Consciousness Raising Committee (Los Angeles). Copyright, 1974. Used by permission of the authors.

The Sensuous Person: Critique and Correction, by Albert Ellis. Copyright, 1972, by Lyle Stuart, Inc. Published by arrangement with Lyle Stuart. Used by permission of the publisher.

Answers to Those Male Chauvinist Putdowns, by the Feminist Invention Group. Copyright, 1973, by Feminist Invention Group, Inc., 333 East 49th Street 8J, New York, NY 10017. Reprinted with permission.

Anger, by Leo Madow. Copyright, 1972, by Leo Madow. Reprinted by permission of Charles Scribner's Sons.

"Chart of Three Fellows We All Know," by Gerald W. Piaget, Ph.D., Behavior Therapy Associates, Los Altos, CA, presented at the Orthopsychiatric Convention in San Francisco, April, 1974. Used by permission of the author.

"Twenty Mile Zone," by Dory Previn. Published by Mediarts Music, Inc./Bouquet Music.© Used by permission of the author.

Peoplemaking, by Virginia Satir. Copyright, 1972, by Science and Behavior Books. Used by permission of the author.

"The Queen Bee Syndrome," by Graham Staines, Carol Tavris and Toby E. Jayaratne, appeared in *Psychology Today,* January, 1974. Used by permission of the authors.

Feel Free, by David S. Viscott. Copyright, 1971, by Wyden Press. Used by permission of Peter H. Wyden Company.

Notes:

Notes:

Notes: